Happiness in your Head

From Hong Kong Banker to Sunny Coast Chancer

GARETH WILLIAMS

Happiness in your Head

tellwell

Tellwell Talent
www.tellwell.ca

ISBN
978-0-2288-8616-7 (Hardcover)
978-0-2288-8615-0 (Paperback)

PREFACE

I have always wanted to write a book.

I have always wanted to have something more to look back on than a linear, corporate career.

I have always sensed that there is a deeper life-journey to be indulged than beaching an exhausted office career onto the shores of a heavily-trailed retirement. And that, only after a journey whose only purpose was to arrive at its destination - having never explored a more adventurous route as my own skipper.

Our advanced technologies gift us unimaginable access to the wisdom, both ancient and modern, beamed to us from celestial bodies – satellites and stars – deep in the night skies to help us navigate humanity's most challenging currents…and the forthcoming storm.

Today, we are more able than ever to plot our own course. To take responsibility for working out which guiding lights to follow.

I am not saying I have got this right. But I have tried. Am trying.

Having broken ranks and jumped overboard (albeit in a family life raft), I am at the early stages of gauging whether our own unique journey will lead us to a more content, fulfilled domain or will see us furiously scramble for the distress flares.

Writing this book goes at least some way towards finding out.

DEDICATION

To My Family

TABLE OF CONTENTS

INTRODUCTION

When asked what surprised him most about humanity, the ***Dalai Lama*** answered:

"Man. Because he sacrifices his health to make money. Then he sacrifices his money to recuperate his health. And then he is so anxious about the future that he does not enjoy the present; the result being that he does not live in the present or the future; he lives as if he is never going to die, then dies having never really lived".

"The Diary of a C*nt".

Immature. Uncouth. Unnecessary. Unlike the Dalai's wise words.

However, for quite some time, as I perennially festered in my mainstream office tedium, I had fantasised about writing my semi-autobiographical memoirs. Like so many of us.

And that had been the title I had landed upon.

I thought it portrayed a playful panache. A snappy caption to catch your eye from the display in your local bookshop.

Indeed, after reading this you may well end up agreeing that the name fits.

Originally, the big idea was to capture a thigh-slapping, slapstick insight into the appalling, alcohol-charged extracurricular behaviours of my early adulthood. A glimpse behind the scenes in London in the 1990s/2000s of one of too many young professionals less than laser-focussed on their careers.

Thankfully, for everyone, those fables of ethanol-perpetuated idiocy, so unique in their far-fetchedness that they defy any accusation of having been confected, have seen their recollection blurred with the onset of middle-age. Perhaps as a result of a subconscious mechanism deep within our psyche, those outrageous storylines that once had us convulsing in stomach-cramped disbelief on a Sunday morning have been gently smudged away. Escapades that had us feverishly assembling a hangover-management lunch to recast, rephrase and relive the previous evening's appalling antics...now forgotten.

But I left it too late. To dial back into focus those tall-but-true tales would require extensive trawling across participants' collective memories, presumably also gently faded by the passing of time.

Now, in place of my four-letter diary, I have a more contemporary tale to tell. My Corona Chronicles – Corona-cles (you are going to have to excuse persistent piss-poor puns…and atrocious alliteration).

Everyone has a COVID story. Far, far too may have heart-breaking experiences that saw victims frogmarched to the extremities of human indignity, sorrow and, in equal measure, fury, anger, rage. All I want to do, is to tell a story. What I hope is an interesting one. I will rant a little, elaborate a little, deckchair-philosophise and possibly even preach.

However, all I am really seeking to do is to divert. To spin a yarn. And, at the very least, leave behind a recollection for our two Boys, Rex and Raf – so that they can see what and how we were thinking as these history-altering events unfolded.

I would like to present a human account of a family that took control over and rewrote their script. We decamped from the routinely trodden foothills and, via an event-laded "World Detour", yomped from Hong Kong to Spain, Croatia to England and, finally, to a new home in Australia.

My story starts at Chinese New Year (January), 2020. The Chinese Year of the Rat. Our family had been living in Hong Kong for five and a half years and we were pretty much still in "loving it" mode. But, before I properly get going, maybe I should first assemble a brief background:

Hi There

This will be a fairly honest account viewed from my perspective. You, dear reader, will most definitely have your own views. Not only on the topics I touch upon but also of me. It would be deluded hubris to think you agree with all that I have to say. Or even to respect it. All that I ask is that you tolerate my thoughts. For it is tolerance that is now in short supply.

I am a bald, white, heterosexual middle-aged man. Not tall nor short. Medium height. Not ripped nor fat. A healthy BMI.

For my sins, and where this story begins, I was a banker.

Notwithstanding the above, I consider myself a good person. A decent chap. Only I know what and how I think. I am very self-reflective and analytical. I am confident that my motives are, 99% of the time, good-natured.

I mean well.

I think the vast majority of us do. We want the same things: people to be able to live in a peaceful, vibrant environment with nourishment, shelter and self-determination. Where most of the differences lie in peoples' views is not in the destination but rather in belief as to what is the optimal means of travel.

I am stubborn and hate to admit I am wrong, especially if you challenge me in the now, confronting…on the spot. If I am going to have to climb down, allow me to slip quietly away from my error and to humbly email you with the face-saving detachment of time and distance!

I took my parents' example to heart of treating everyone the same, from a Lord to a layman, a prince to a pauper, a pisshead to a puritan, etc. Take each person as they come and start by assuming the best of people. And that there is always something you can learn from any person.

Most people in the modern West would describe my politics as markedly right-wing. Right-wing nowadays is seen as a harsh, selfish, profit-obsessed mentality.

That's not me. I think a lot about this labelling versus principles mismatch. I wonder why the positions I take as being morally and ethically the best tend to coincide with those allocated to the right-wing camp. I want the world to be a better place and passionately seek the elimination of poverty, war, recrimination, graft, corruption, environmental degradation etc, etc. As does every sane human being.

But from a young age I saw clearly that there are always trade-offs. It's not enough to want something. Actions have positive and negative consequences, many of them unforeseen. And this is where I gravitate to the facts versus feelings path, which roughly translates to the heuristic for badging someone right- (facts) versus left-wing (feelings).

I was grateful for *Jonathan Haidt* drilling into these questions brilliantly in his book, *The Righteous Mind.* Whilst everyone bar psycho- and sociopaths wants a more peaceful, collaborative, happier world I consider some of the more important traits in achieving that to be loyalty and accountability. Traits, he posits, that are reflective of the "right".

Haidt argues that someone on the "left" would focus more on fairness. However, I find that the concept of "fairness" incredibly difficult to pin down and, to a material extent, leads back to questions of loyalty and accountability.

We all seek the same goals and just see different paths and values to reaching them.

Despite the above, I think the whole left/right categorisation is something of a failed construct and that the dichotomy that is now emerging is centralised, top-down enforcement versus bottom-up trust in the aggregation of individual, sovereign behaviours.

We have seen the desire for more government warp through political space-time to marry up with massively powerful, crony-capitalist corporations.

But more about that later!

I am half Welsh and half German. I think, as a result, I see the concept of intergenerational blame as utterly dismissible stupidity and, indeed, the route to a lot of unnecessary evil.

These trendy concepts of humans of a certain characteristic (white, male, heterosexual) being inherently guilty of an "ism" is pseudo-intellectual trash. It is indicative of a society which has become so complacently comfortable that it has forgotten how to think about the bigger questions in life. It has started to consume itself with peripheral quarrels and micro-gripes.

I have always loved writing. Up until the last couple of years my enjoyable writing has been restricted to pithy work emails and the occasional team updates for friends and family.

I have always loved words. How they sound. Their rhythm. How they elide, interlink or clash. How we can sew together a combination of marks on paper to create a reaction inside the minds of others – unbounded by geography. And over millennia. Without physically sensing what is being communicated, inked markings on paper tease your mind into recognising the concepts, sensations and even revelations being conveyed. Words can deliver impact. Like a slap, flat across the cheek, with a solid slab of fresh haddock.

I have always loved my late father's mantra: "you can't take life too seriously". Tragically, he took this message a step too far by ignoring the early signs of bowel cancer. But the underlying message stands. I am known to lose my footing on the precipitous cliff of making light of the wrong occasion, but I do firmly believe too many people take themselves too seriously. In fact, it is the result of some seriously unserious individuals taking themselves and their megalomaniac ideologies too seriously that is in danger of dragging us into a future hellish mire.

I have enjoyed the ultimate blessing of an extremely close and loving family. I never heard my parents swap a mean word and can count on the fingers of one hand the number of times my father raised his voice to me.

I can't remember my mother being angry once.

Being a father of two boys, aged seven and nine, this blows my mind.

My parents worked hard in their medic professions and sacrificed enough to put me through a private English education that saw me emerge with a decent haul of exam grades but with very little idea of what I wanted to do with them.

I did what the system asked of me. I conformed, I rote-learned, I passed exams so that I would have the opportunity to pass more exams...to obtain qualifications that would allow me to rent out my services to a large corporate. A career.

I approached the transitions from school to university and university to corporate very much bedded in that jolly mindset: you strive to rent out your time and effort to a major institution in return for a wage, security and a career path.

Entrepreneurship was a foreign word. It might as well have been French. The insane idea of trying something on your own was wantonly reckless – irresponsible - to the point of creating a family intervention!

In this environment, I dutifully studied economics at a red brick university and made it onto the graduate course at a large accounting firm. I look back longingly with a regretful nausea at how little, during those prime years of education, any intellectual curiosity was encouraged out of its sleepy cage. Rather than being set free to frolic and playfully bump heads, it was confined and fed minimum rations.

Joining a graduate scheme and qualifying as an accountant in London financial services was an extension of university. The program was populated by many other under-matured graduates. Yes, we studied properly hard for exams and worked long hours, but it was the embodiment of the cliché, work-hard-play-hard.

In those days pre-2008, banking was seen as a cerebral profession for the ethical and wise (I shit you not) and it was what every accountant wanted to do after qualifying. That status came with the added bonus of promises of great riches (in return for the best years of your life). I joined a major European bank in 2000. From my London base I slowly built my career and, like the cogs ticking over in a watch, notched week after week, clocking-up year after year.

The Fam

It had been during one of the quieter Saturday pub evenings in one of these seven-day loops that I had met my Australian wife, Kate.

I had spent an unhealthy amount of time over the previous decades seeking my "FMW" (Future Mrs Williams). But that is a different story and one that belongs under the diary title mentioned previously.

Suffice to say that Fate finally played her hand and arranged for me to be on the right side of the sliding doors that evening. My hither-to-that-moment unsuccessful search had led me to believe that there was no such thing as love at first sight. Rather there is lust at first sight that happens to morph into love. And that is what I so fortuitously stumbled upon that night.

Maybe as a function of the loving family in which I had grown up, I had always wanted to have children…to be a father. As my personal clock ticked over into the second half of my 30s, I was overwhelmingly happy to have found the person with whom I wanted to spend the rest of my life.

Driven by that passionate enthusiasm purring under the bonnet of a 37-year-old wannabe father, we married and had our first son, Rex, before I hit 40.

So: husband and father; a decent-sized terraced house in Battersea; a predictable banking career tracking through the horizon into a rosy future. I had found a regular weekly routine that had grown into a familiar, mesmeric drumbeat of a comfortable living.

Weekly cycles of five days' work plus two days' play. Annual cycles punctuated with skiing and summer holidays, annual bonuses and the passing of the British seasons.

Then, confrontingly and after 20 years, in 2014 I was presented with the opportunity of doing something other than stacking another 20 years on top of the 20 I had already amassed in London's traditional, perma-suited banking sector.

There was a role coming up in Hong Kong and I was the preferred choice. The question was posed: keep ticking over or change it all.

Some readers may recognise how easy it is to slot into a mid-life groove of effectively looping the same commute, restaurants and friends whilst gently coveting an ever more favourable asset versus future expense ratio. Socialising was effortless – you knew there would always be someone available for a drink or a bite to eat as soon as you passed the Wednesday midweek hump of the office schedule.

Kate is a fiercely independent Queenslander with a no-nonsense farming family, the McNicholls, that collectively embrace all things rural, green and natural. So, a chancing of the arm at a life in Hong Kong seemed to me to be a proposition that would likely be disdainfully batted back.

But no. After a colluding huddle with the broader McNicholl tribe, the white smoke surprisingly emerged. My theory then (yes, and now) was that this transition was seen as Step I of shifting closer to the

Mothership Australia and that the classified plans for Step II were already under construction.

Anyway, after a lot of performative umming and ahhhing, the clinching question of, "what will it feel like to never know what could have been" won the day and we upped sticks, bade our farewells and made for Honkers Bonkers. The ummming and ahhhing had provided sufficient opportunity to allow for number two son, Raf, to be gently gestating away as we took off for Asia.

Heat Shock

I had never properly understood what people meant by culture shock. Everywhere is different and it requires a powerful failure of imagination or empathy not to realise that anywhere other than Battersea is going to be different to Battersea. But it was not so much culture that caught us out.

Kate and I had consulted broadly on the pros and cons of moving to Hong Kong and the ridiculousness of the weather had been made clear by enough people for us to take it seriously. But words alone did not prepare us for arriving in mid-May with one 20-month-old boy and a wife, belly-nursing the second, into what was a wall of 35c, 95% humidity. Four steps into the outside oven and niggly beads of perspiration are scurrying down the nape of your neck. After ten steps, they overcome your eyebrow defences and make for the inner eye… ten steps further and you sweatily surrender, shamelessly conceding the appearance of someone who has been dunked in a paddling pool.

The heat made it feel dangerous to allow Rex to spend more than 15 minutes in the playground. His expression of blank amazement, blotched with reddening cheeks, signalled he was nearing his outdoor limits. However, the alternative of our sealed and cooled temporary apartment, with its windows weeping condensation, imposed the strong sense of being contained inside a chiller cabinet.

Outside bad. Inside also bad.

Anyway, after a tricky start getting up and running and with the early months spent focussing on the Asian birth of Raf, we set about making Hong Kong our home.

And we grew very much to love it.

There is no doubt that the expat lifestyle in Hong Kong is starkly different to most. Both the expat bit and the Hong Kong bit. It is, undoubtedly, privileged.

The two Boys grew up in complete safety (next to zero street crime). We had help cleaning and washing from our (live out) helper. Despite our original determined intention to avoid hiring/exploiting external help in constructing our household, it became clear to us that running a household in Hong Kong was going to be a relationship-damaging challenge. I have had to listen to myself trying to explain to hard-working parents in the UK juggling the blizzard of tasks that come with combining work and bringing up children, how it's "different" in Hong Kong…and I sound so painfully lame that I peter out into an embarrassed, shame-faced mumble.

So, I won't do that here beyond musing that the entire expat infrastructure was built on the assumption that everyone had help. Suffice to say, that we were lucky enough to have that help.

We also managed to score a deeply treasured membership at the Hong Kong Cricket Club…oh, oasis of grass, beer and beautifully banal banter. This was not without some self-sacrifice on my part, mind. My corporate membership turned out to be a false promise (a downright whopper). My bank essentially said, sorry, we lied. And so, I was forced to put my aging cricketing skills to the test in the team trials that take place every August. I was, at best, in the middle of a pack of 60 contenders for the 10 spots available in the teams. That, together with what I gathered was a tight-knit. Antipodean mafia with unabated nepotistic tendencies meant that I fell well short.

However, there was a need for another scorer.

So, on behalf of my family, I went from Botham-like allrounder to geeky statto.

But it was worth it.

At the same time as my cricketing career cratered, my working one had inched in the right direction, being promoted to a highly visible role in charge of a team across Asia Pacific. Kate had acted as our ambassador for friendship and we had developed a terrific circle of friends. Having only ever expected to last in Hong Kong for three years, come Chinese New Year 2020, we were asking ourselves whether it would be seven or eight…or nine…

Yet, all the time, Kate and I shared a sense that we were not living the lives that we wanted to live…that we would be proud of. We were 100% grateful for the experience and would not change it for the world. But we knew that longer term, our family's contentment would require change. Hong Kong presented a privileged lifestyle. One that did not capture the full spectrum of what we felt Rex and Raf needed to experience. We both sensed we needed to exit the bubble to provide the Boys with the chance to grow up with broader, grounded perspectives and surrounded by nature.

Well – that's the background.

PART I - THE DECISION TO TRANSITION
Hong Kong

"Every man has two lives and the second starts when he realizes he has just one."

Confucius

Chinese New Year 2020

January 2020 had seen a gentle start to the year. We had arrived back from a Christmas in the UK with my lovely family and were slotting back into our Hong Kong routines. Over the previous weeks there had already been disseminated some low-level news snippets surrounding a virus in China. However, the reports had been buried deep enough in the local newspapers that the story was only germinating in the subconscious of most people.

It was over the weekend of the Chinese New Year that the story barged itself to the number one current affairs topic.

On Thursday 23rd January I was lucky enough to be the Mystery Reader for Raf's class at his international school. This involved hiding in a side room to his class before making a celebrity emergence and delivering an over-acted (and over-gory, come to think of it) version of the Greek Myths to him and his school friends. Little was I to know that was to be the last time I would be inside the school.

The Friday night heralded the start of the celebratory four-day weekend extended by the two public holidays to welcome in the Chinese Year of the Rat. Cue a lot of the expat mates excitedly meeting up for post-work beers. We started off with table service beers at a popular joint called Wagyu before the emulsifying effects of strong continental lager saw us diffusing and draining into the random watering holes dotted around the complex plumbing of Lang Kwai Fong.

If it wasn't necessarily the number one topic of the evening, the coronavirus (as it was then being called) was certainly in the top billing. I clearly remember (must have been early in the evening) being shown a photo of some chap on an airplane wearing a mask and a rain poncho as protection. He was dismissed as a hypochondriac nutter but one could sense a background glimmer of foreboding.

That was the last pre-COVID congregation. That was the before. Everything since has been the after.

As I was feeling a little "dusty" (Hong Kong expat slang for hungover) the next day, early morning cricket being cancelled for the boys was far from a disaster. The immediacy of WhatsApp ensured that the news quickly spread that numerous events were being cancelled as a precaution. The ubiquitous feeling was, let's be careful – this could be very serious. Naturally, there was a collective muscle-memory in Hong Kong of the SARS outbreak in 2003 and this allowed an automatic switching to those precautions that had been implemented for that virus.

Without any public instruction, masks we almost universally adorned, hand-sanitisers appeared on all available flat surfaces and temperature guns were levelled at willingly submissive entrants to restaurants, shops and offices.

The four-day weekend celebration became a much more muted affair, although we still teamed up with a number of other couples for a BBQ on the Monday evening.

Initial Reaction

Wednesday 29th January would have been the first day of the Year of the Rat back in the office, but everyone had been advised to work from home ("WFH"). WFH was brand new territory in Hong Kong. Unlike in other parts of the world where individuals were accommodated and – amazingly – even encouraged to WFH, in Hong Kong it was unambiguously deemed to be skiving. In addition, with astronomic rents per square metre, no-one really had the room at home to spare to make up an office. No re-purposed sheds in the back garden for the Kowloon commuters.

So WFH was a novelty. As was on-line learning for the kids, as opposed to face-to-face schooling.

Thankfully, this combustible clash of all four of us attending to our daily tasks in the same apartment only lasted for the three remaining days of the week. Making and clearing breakfast whilst coaxing a five- and seven-year-old into their respective virtual Zoom classrooms before a 9am conference call on the latest under-priced Green Loan was not a routine that promised long term serenity.

Fortuitously, we had previously planned (pre-COVID, as is now a catchphrase for delineating what will be a permanent societal shift) for Kate and the Lads to head over to her family in Australia for a two-week visit.

Departure

I took Kate and the Boys to the airport on the Sunday evening. We were concerned enough about the virus for Kate to have prepared a fistful of homemade antiseptic wipes (tissues soaked in Dettol) for the drive. I feverishly scrubbed my hands as we accelerated away from the unavoidable highway toll booths having reluctantly accepted clammy coin change.

It was a surreal moment, as I tried to zoom out of the scene at the airport drop-off. I don't want to over-dramatise the moment, but my hollow stomach signalled the same sensation as when reading stories of wartime child evacuees.

5½ year old Raf was bawling at full lung capacity, being made to wear a mask for the first time in his life. Kate was trying to put her arm around both Rex and Raf whilst simultaneously wheeling the luggage trolley through the automatic entrance doors.

I wondered how this was going to play out, as the shambolic trio veered out of sight for what was still conceived as a two-week holiday.

Little was I to know that they would not return to Hong Kong for five months.

I had planned to follow Kate and the Boys two weeks later. In the meantime, I slipped into a locked-down bachelor routine that was to become hypnotically familiar.

From the very beginning, I had been monitoring developments in Wuhan closely. There was a Twitter feed that would update each morning on the number of infections in China and a check on this was the first action I would take each morning. A concoction of emotions amounting to awe and foreboding would well inside each morning as I woke up to news that the numbers had again increased…each time by an increased increment.

At the same time, Twitter was abuzz with rumours: videos of body bags, mid-walk collapses, prefabricated hospitals built in days and columns of hazmat-suited fumigators disinfecting streets…somewhere. I would like to say that I was dismissively sceptical at the time of this Twitter-fare. But I was not. A wide-eyed compulsion instructed me to gather as much information from as many sources as possible in order to make sense of this.

The commencement of my coronavirus obsession?

Maybe – but it was certainly coming from the angle that this was something to worry about.

On Podcasts

I can't remember exactly when I first started listening to podcasts. Certainly, I was stressing about downloading the BBC's Wake Up to Money in time to head off to work when I was still in London in the early 2010s. I loved them straight away, avoiding any issues about timing and radio reception. And it is fair to say that I am an unashamed podcast addict.

More than that: I am an addicted advocate. I dearly love and treasure them. They have opened my mind to incredibly valuable realms of thought that I truly think would have otherwise remained hidden.

Our industrial education system is insanely narrow. Hopelessly rooted in static information as opposed to fluid knowledge. Gloriously vibrant pools of ancient wisdom are utterly neglected in preference for temporarily memorising facts.

Podcasts allow you to pick and choose what topics to pipe into your mind, what areas to explore...with discussions and debates constructed based on the whole cumulative available thought/work/practice/science of humanity.

Just think about it: you get to listen to individuals who have dedicated their professional lives to absorbing all they can about whatever topic you have stumbled upon or selected. You can listen to the two most eminent experts on Platonic/Stoic/Aristotelian/Marxist philosophy, the history of the gold standard, Younger Dryas Period, hallucinogenic mushrooms, Pearl Harbour, joke-making, Keynesianism versus Austrian school of economics, neuroscience, evolutionary biology, etc, etc.

So, you have the millennia of human experience, science, philosophy studied over a lifetime by dedicated experts to be debated in your ears at your convenience. Giants standing on the shoulders of Titans. At your ready disposal.

That's before you listen in on pundits picking apart current affairs from polar-opposite perspectives.

I love them.

And I wonder how different my path might have been if I had access to this resource from a younger age.

Podcasts have touched upon enduring truths, clarified or organised deep contemplations I had been dwelling on in an isolated ignorance of what had already been philosophised. Sufficiently so, that they have changed my approach to life. Or rather, nursed those nascent notions to a level of strength sufficient to enact real changes.

They snapped me out of a hypnotic, complacent and ultimately empty way of living. I have come to understand myself better. I now have a more powerful grip on what I want from life.

It is no exaggeration to state the podcasts that have caught my attention have been responsible for asserting in me a renewed confidence in my core principles and values. For what will deliver more meaning in life.

Hong Kong Bachelor

I touched upon just how fiercely the Hong Kong furnace can fire up in the summer. Over the years this had led to the clichéd but unavoidable emergence of the "Hong Kong Bachelor". This phenomenon emanates from the hostility of the summer blaze, combined with vacant weeks of July and August laid bare by school holidays. In addition, most expat parents naturally want to touch base with their parents across the globe. So, mothers (typically) would take their offspring to European / US / Australian climes and leave their industrious husbands behind to manfully mine the office rockface…and manage those yawning weekend voids as best they could.

The early weeks of COVID restrictions in Hong Kong did not see anything like the jabberingly crazy lockdowns that the hysterically panicky West would shortly inflict in concert. However, the concern became real enough for families to keep themselves to themselves. I was happy enough to find company in the occasional FaceTime calls with my family...and with podcast after podcast dissecting what I recognised early on would be historically significant events.

So, whilst the typical Hong Kong bachelor weekends would create golden opportunities for long, lazy afternoons of gentle beerdom, I found myself putting together a more solo schedule that involved bloody-minded hiking all over Hong Kong Island.

Hong Kong, it is worth pointing out, is in fact a very green, jungle-like island. Large parts of it are undeveloped and criss-crossed with hiking trails that allow you to feel that you have escaped the concreted claustrophobia of the city and to have ventured into lush rain forest.

As a result, hiking had unexpectedly become a favourite pastime. Especially with the discovery of ever more fascinating podcasts, I would try to grab an hour or two to dehydrate myself trekking a nearby loop up 1,300 steps (known as "The Twins") and home along the catchwater.

Now, in the temporary absence of my family, the weekends offered the chance to take this to another level and I duly committed myself to four-hour sweatathons. To help combat the draining loss of liquids, I found certain hike-hacks that took some of the edge off the self-inflicted demands, such as putting ice-blocks into my water backpack, a towel to dry hands in order to be able to operate my phone and a HKD 100 note...just in case exhaustion forced me to take a taxi home.

Perhaps it is a result of my Teutonic genes that I have always had a mindset that revels in reward but only to the extent that I have endured strain, struggle or suffering that justifies it. Historically, Friday night after a long working week. A two-week holiday after a marathon vacation-free stint in the office. And in Hong Kong I found I would enjoy downtime by a factor of multiples if I had pushed myself to the point of heat exhaustion before indulging in food, wine and television.

After a 20km hike in an outdoor sauna, my go-to was an evening, beer-accompanied foot massage plus dinner plus sofa combo.

That may sound odd. But it's worth noting that in Hong Kong foot massages were very much a thing. Kate and I (and we were by no means the only couple) had made it a regular centrepiece of our date nights. Time-permitting there was the 90-minute option during which one could torment oneself over whether to allocate time to reading, sleeping, podcasting or concentrating on the massage itself. Quite often I found the stress of selecting one of these options overwhelming the joy of the massage.

Whilst mildly uncomfortable, the silence-fracturing "tsch" heralding the opening of my third can of craft ale (they are Bring Your Own alcohol massages!) and the accompanying side-glances from fellow massagees and masseuses was a price I was flatly happy to pay.

The foot massage parlours were dark, contemplative venues so, on emergence, I would blink in the remaining light of the dusk. Contentedly shuffling into the nearby Japanese Yakitori restaurant for an indulgent meal for one, I would usually be the first diner of the evening. This was with a view to eating early and maximising sofa time.

Whilst this would not be my preferred "route to midnight" on a Saturday evening, I had always enjoyed dining on my own and so was able to adapt to the weekend isolation forced upon me at the early stages of the plandemic with ease.

Once on the sofa, my TV viewing would gradually deteriorate as Sunday morning reluctantly took over the baton from Saturday night. I would lose the precise thread of some of the more intricate arguments on YouTube and become increasingly frustrated with the inexactness of the rewind function on the remote control. Eventually, I would slide grinningly into watching Led Zeppelin, Radiohead, Sisters of Mercy and Stone Roses videos...and, of course, Freebird.

Aaaaaaand beddy-byes!

Awesome. My COVID routine. And to some of the boys reading this, I suspect you could use a bit of Hong Kong Bachelordom. However, and I am saying this absent a nervous glance out of the corner of my eye to gauge whether the Mrs is judging, after a week or two…it does become a little empty. Maybe it would have been less so, in the times when it was easier to meet up and go out-out. But even then, it blows my mind how much time kids absorb. And how much time you are happy for them to absorb.

Suddenly, there were open stretches of hours not pre-allocated to cooking, entertaining, shopping, tidying, playdate taxi-ing, cricket lessons, etc, etc.

I am a person who yearns for a bit of me-time. But a day, OK probably two, is enough. I like to kick ideas about with friends and family. Quite usually to a point beyond irritation. After a particularly interesting news article, podcast or book, I turn into that child who has come home from an adventure weekend and just hoses forth all the new ideas/experiences he thinks are so uniquely interesting.

Anyway, suffice to say that Hong Kong Bachelordom should only ever be enjoyed in small bursts – always time limited. The special administrative region is littered with (mostly Anglos-Saxon) expats who Pre-COVID overindulged in this way of life and who, as a result, are unlikely to be able to fully integrate back into normal, civilised society.

I wonder how they are getting on now? With the continuing domination of Hong Kong by the CCP and the need for skilled labour in the West, maybe there is an increasing business need for an expat rehabilitation program!

MuteTube

All the time I was reading, watching and listening to everything I could on what the WHO had now decreed should be called COVID-19. My interest and suspicion had already been piqued by what I perceived as a scandalous mismatch between what the data were indicating and what the media was reporting.

But that suspicion was pushed forcefully towards an ever-greater certainty as I saw the flat-out contradictions.

We all know that the lab leak "theory" is now mainstream. However, I remember making the point to a colleague that the unequivocal contradiction by the CDC (Fauci) on mask-wearing could not be denied. Now, you could (although, I really wish you wouldn't!) argue that it was a "noble lie" and that masks were always a materially beneficial precaution. That the reason that the CDC decided to lie nobly was to preserve PPE stocks for medical staff. However, you cannot argue that the CDC didn't lie. They said you absolutely do not need them and then said that you must wear them. So how many statements since have been noble lies? And who gets to decide which lies are noble.

There are always trade-offs.

And THEN YouTube tangled itself in knots by saying it would censor any information that was against (current?) public health advice.

So, they were having to delete the CDC's own contradictory original message?

It amazed me how few people saw this as a red flag. As well as the deletion of alternate views.

In April 2020 I watched a very convincing and heartfelt video from two Californian doctors whose message was "plenty of cases, very few deaths". Essentially, they were saying that the COVID-19 disease was mostly an issue for the already susceptible...that it was not an issue that warranted shutting down countries. This matched my reading of the data.

What they were saying might or might not have been true. But when I looked up the video a few days later, it had been taken down by the YouTube censors.

Now – you can marshal information in the MSM all you want but preventing me from listening to the first-hand experience of front-line doctors is not going to seal the argument for me.

At the same time the analysis of hitherto World-leading Stanford professor and expert epidemiologist, John Ioannidis, demonstrating that the danger of COVID was much less than was being broadly portrayed was being ignored and dismissed – in a systemic fashion.

October 2020 saw the blatant censoring of the Great Barrington Declaration. Googling, "The Great Barrington Declaration" the results would only show the link to the Great Barrington Declaration website on the second page of results. Shocking.

The zenith of this self-defeating curation of the "truth" was the censoring of Dr Pierre Kory's senate testimony on treatments and repurposed drugs in December 2020.

Permission, per-lease

I suspect a few of you have that boss who, when they concede a point – anything – even something that they have zero option but to concede to maintain any outward semblance of integrity, does so in a way that is somehow begrudging and designed to re-emphasise their control or power over you?

That's how my boss eventually acquiesced to my passionate request to visit my family in Australia. I proposed to work from hotel quarantine for two weeks, take two weeks holiday and "work from abroad" for a further two weeks before heading back to Hong Kong. Bear in mind, that most people were working remotely at this stage, so the only real concerns were time zone (two hours' difference) and internet strength. But I was made to testify to my (untested) internet access in Australia as well as dedication to working all hours god sends.

I don't want to go into too much detail about my boss. There is less than a handful of people that, when I hear their name, my neural connections to trigger a reflexive clench.

It has been a widely held debate as to whether you have to be a bit of a sociopath to hold senior positions in a global bank or large corporate. I have certainly seen exceptions: genuinely good people who have combined intelligence, kindness and resilience to reach lofty positions in corporations. But they are the exceptions. You have to be a flawed narcissist to accept the political surrenders you just have to make to navigate your way through the artificial, often whimsical power pathways to promotion.

My analogy might be that of a children's early learning toy – it consists of different shaped blocks (circles, squares, triangles, etc) that the child needs to push through the equivalent openings on the wooden surface of a cube. To reach a high position in a company you have to fit through all those differently-shaped slots. You have to whittle away the corners and edges that make you, your shape. You have to become an amorphous little pellet that slides through every arbitrary aperture to access the inner cube.

Or you have to be the bully that smashes up the toy entirely.

A bit of a tortured metaphor but you take the point.

Anyway, I was conditionally granted permission to head to Australia to see my family after four weeks of sanity-testing, locked-down Hong Kong Bachelordom!

Private Jumbo Jet

Arriving at the Virgin check-in desk for my flight to Brisbane, I thought I had properly screwed up. For a long time, there was no-one there. No-one. No passenger, no staff…no-one in the entire check-in hall.

It was marginally re-assuring, half an hour in, to witness a busload of workers file through the monolithic check-in atrium but only marginally.

After a painfully long time hopping from foot to foot whilst aimlessly tapping in my phone's passcode, another passenger arrived. She was a barrister, I was powerfully informed. And had a similar level of confidence as me as to what was going on.

As it turned out, we formed two thirds of the passengers scheduled on this long-haul Dreamliner 787 flight to Brisbane. I have photos of the flight, row after row, section after section of empty seats.

The crew outnumbered us by a factor of three or four and they were incredibly friendly. I spoke to one for an hour about how she knew she was about to be made redundant as a result of reduced flights due to the shamdemic.

By this stage, I had already clambered above the frenzied fog of COVID hysteria and was constantly trying to weigh up how honest to be and in which situations with my views: what does this person think, can I be bothered to have the argument right here, right now. If I do, will it change anything, etc.

The crew took a gentle and well-meant delight in the lucky-dip moment of truth that accompanied the opening of the plane doors on arrival in

Brisbane. They had informed us that this was the moment we would be notified of our allocated hotel for our two weeks of enforced solo detention. The entire passenger content of the Dreamliner, all three of us, knew that the potentially life-changing experience of being isolated in a hotel room for the next two weeks would be greatly fashioned by the identity of the hotel. There had been both fist-clenching horror stories in the press and on social media as well as more comforting blogs on more benign experiences. Some quarantinees even had balconies!

As the messenger at the door figuratively stuck their hand in a bucket, pulled out and unscrewed a ball of paper, the announcement was made: The Marriott. The three of us simultaneously started furiously tapping on our phones. No balconies, godammit. But, hey, the Marriott. It could certainly have been worse.

Quaran-me time

At this time, Easter 2020, the idea of being isolated in a hotel room without being allowed outside of the door for two weeks was still a stark novelty for the law-abiding in the Western World. It was a favourite conversational thought experiment to brainstorm condiments to bring, books to read, jigsaws to complete. People worried about the food, claustrophobia and lack of sun or exercise.

However, I quite enjoyed my quarantine. I don't know if that's a popular view or not. But it ticked quite a few boxes for me:

- It was a new experience and challenge;
- It held out a great reward at its completion (seeing my family);
- It was free (!);
- It would provide a (since diluted) dinner party anecdote for the future to make me sound more interesting;
- It thrust upon me unallocated time (to read, to meditate);

- I still spoke to friends, family and colleagues for large chunks of the day;
- I was able to deliver a market review to my work colleagues whilst sat in the buff (just because).

I don't think I have been in a more efficient work environment. Australian TV is just so witlessly dull that it turns itself off. Seriously, I can find myself getting roped into some very average viewing, but this fare was of such bland nothingness that it was more pleasurable to sit in silence and stare out of the window.

So, during the working week, I would kick off by doing some exercise. The room was 12 paces long and I would chalk-up shuttle runs / walks for hours. I would feed podcast after podcast through my travel speaker and lose myself in the discussions whilst shuffling from the door to the window, window to the door...again and again.

I would action any emails, calls or pieces of writing with a clear-minded, execution-driven focus (WITHOUT INTERRUPTIONS) that meant they were completed quickly and well. Leaving more time for step-accumulation, riveting podcast insights and reading.

I was averaging over 20,000 steps a day. It was the first time since my youth (maybe ever) that I would read for four hours in a row... WITHOUT INTERRUTIONS!

It was like being a modern-day monk but without all the weird stuff!

I did try to meditate. It was strange, in that I had been wanting to give it a proper try for a long, long time and very clearly two weeks of enforced isolation was going to provide the perfect opportunity. But I still found it difficult to make myself do it. I don't know why. When I did, I used Sam Harris's ten-minute introduction that he issued for free yonks ago. I got into it and I think I may have fallen asleep (I hadn't checked the time before starting). I enjoyed it. But I haven't done it since.

On the food front, it started well. I would even concede that I was delivered food that surpassed my expectations. But it quickly became samey. And, with increasing regularity, would be delivered cold.

Cold both in the sense of temperature as well as human interaction that came with it. *Yes*, I understood that the whole point was to isolate me for fear of transmission of the virus…*but* would it really be so difficult to say, "you're welcome!" after I acknowledged the purposeful double-knock on the door with my most friendly-sung "thank you"? Does it really compromise COVID security to say a word or two to acknowledge my acknowledgment?!

Unfriendly silence was the only response.

Anyway, I made it to about day 10 before finally, limply succumbing to Deliveroo. And once that had happened, it was a daily event. Theron in, wide-eyed in front of the laptop, I devoured the colourful choices cheerfully crowding my computer screen as part of the ordering process.

On the booze front, I was an unusually good boy. None whatsoever before the weekend. This was in stark contrast to one of my two fellow Virgin travellers, the Barrister, who had made a great fuss about being able to have her alcohol delivered to her room even as we were transiting from the airport to the hotel.

I felt an utterly misplaced sense of worthy superiority when I heard the daily clanking of her empties being dutifully evacuated from her next-door room. Pious twat, Gareth.

Release

On parting from my room, I self-diagnosed with mild Stockholm Syndrome. Maybe there is a part of our monkey-mind that clicks in when we need to bunker down and just get through on our own?

Given an external imposition of isolation - be it by way of authoritarian rulers or natural disasters - with fixed parameters and the promise of future release, is there part of our survival instinct that overrides with a survival frame of mind? Is this why so many across the globe took to lockdowns with frightening, determined aplomb?

By the end of our World Detour, I ended up being quarantined on my own in a hotel in Brisbane, on my own at home in Hong Kong, with the family at home in Hong Kong, in my mother's UK back garden in September sunshine and finally with the family in a hotel unit in Sydney. I really enjoyed each of those stints in their own particular way. I would even say that I am a more rounded person (I hesitate to say "better" – time will tell) as a result of those experiences. They have shown me how easy it is to adapt and how much simpler we can make our lives.

However, that sense of regretful parting soon dissipated when I left the air-conditioned confines of the Marriott. And that was the main difference that struck me. I hadn't missed the sensation on the cheek of a fresh breeze until the moment I felt it again. And then I retrospectively missed it with a passion. Could that be a life-lesson that it is only after the fact that we realise what we were missing?

It was a gloriously, sun-blessed and very still morning in Brisbane but it was that stroke of nature, that most gentle of micro touches at the end-point of a global weather system that struck me as the most significant reclamation of freedom.

That and seeing the fam, of course! Life-affirming cuddles from the Boys and a family-friendly pash with the Mrs justified the journey to Australia in an instant.

We found a café that was open in the otherwise dystopically evacuated Brisbane CBD. Ahhh, Aussie coffee...(not the instant stuff which I had inflicted on my First World sensibilities under quarantine). But here around us, or rather not around us, was another enormous group of intelligent, strong-minded people with access to the same information as me that accepted the public messaging at face value. Trusting in the fatuous phrase, Trust the Science.

I like to think of myself as a very self-critical person. I think about my behaviour, how I might come across, almost perpetually. I catch myself verbally berating myself, like a drunk tramp, whilst walking along the pavement when an embarrassing memory seeps back into the forefront of my thinking. I ask myself the questions, why have I taken certain positions on issues. I interrogate myself as to whether I am searching for or selecting the arguments that back up the position I have already taken. Have I overextended my neck on another issue? What evidence would change my mind?

Thinking Fast and Slow by *Daniel Kahneman* was an eye-opening read for assessing how we think and how we think we think. And how to think about how we think. I am not suggesting that my belief structures are bias-resistant because I read a book. I can too often sense myself warmly ushering in my biases and wallowing in listening to or reading others articulating the same angles.

However, I do make myself listen to the other side of arguments. Maybe I do this to rehearse / prepare the counterarguments. But I do find myself thinking, no – that's a fair point, or – that's true, I agree with that.

I do try.

Lockdown Rant

But come on.

This whole lockdown psy-op horseshit is of the lowest, maggot-ridden quality.

This isn't going to be a rant that reference studies and weighs up costs versus benefits. Anyone who is interested enough (and I have been somewhat obsessive) can assemble their own factoid troops and have a never-ending argument about which statistics say what.

However, the implementation of lockdown is such self-evident bollocks that its synchronous, undebated imposition across the (mostly) Western World can only mean that it has been coordinated and orchestrated with other goals in mind.

Combine this with the breath-taking level of intelligence-insulting censorship and it just seems clear as day that something is badly wrong.

If you screw up your eyes, clench your fists and really, really wish it to be maybe you could invoke Hanlon's Razor (never put down to malice what you could also attribute to stupidity). But in doing so, you would have to believe that:

- They didn't know the PCR tests were phooey;
- They didn't know that deaths were being systematically over-counted/reported;
- That they genuinely believed humans can fight a war against an airborne virus;
- That it was in our best interests not to hear from better qualified experts with opposing views;
- That the lies they admitted they told us were OK because they were noble lies;
- That the fear campaigns they commissioned and paid for with your money were for the greater good; and
- That masking children is a net benefit to society.

I might come back to some of that later!

So, we drove back to our house in the hinterland of the Sunshine Coast. A family of four, re-united. In the five weeks since we had been parted,

Kate and the Boys had settled in to a new, non-Hong Kong lifestyle. Rex and Raf had, being in possession of Australian passports, enrolled in the local school. It was a charmingly organic junior school, tucked in the midst of verdant Queensland flora on the brow of a 30km incline into the Coral Sea. The Boys were wearing broad-brimmed hats and fizzed with enthusiasm as they waited impatiently to be ferried to school in the mornings...and they were making friends.

They were very happy.

Transition Decision

Kate, I think, knew before I arrived. I subconsciously made my mind up within the first couple of days.

Of course, we had talked about what was transpiring in Hong Kong. With the National Security Law ("NSL") and school closures. We had talked about the need for the Boys to be able to lay down roots. Also for us. The path of least resistance was to tick over in Hong Kong for as long as we could. But we both knew it was not the life we wanted to live any longer. The question was either to grow as a family as expats in Hong Kong...or in the blossoming nature of the Sunshine Coast hinterland.

There was only ever going to be one answer.

Whilst there would be a tangled jungle of matters to machete through, we would leave Hong Kong and bring the boys to the Sunny Coast - to provide them with the environment in which they could deeply, properly immerse themselves and their childhoods.

I would terminate my 27-year career in finance. I would find something new and rewarding in the local community.

This is where I am a bad man: I knew instinctively that living outside Montville, bathed in warm sun, nestled in green foliage and with an outdoor, happy upbringing there for the taking was what was best for the family. But I needed to indulge in the early of stages of grief first!

No more free champagne in the Cathay business lounge (at that time, we thought business flights might be back on the cards within months), no more empty-but-nice status, being able to extinguish daily admin fires by dousing them with money. No more Hong Kong Cricket Club, foot massages. No more Hunanese food, no more sauna-hikes. Being able to dot around Asia Pacific for mini breaks. No more being equidistant between Kate's family and mine.

No more bonuses. Severely depleted financial fire power.

A necessary untangling of a mindset that viewed my work as security.

I can remember the realisation sinking in, as Kate and I each had a glass of rosé at the Noosa surf club. We had just skootched down the 30km embankment to the beach for an afternoon, post-school play in the tumbling waves and were talking happily about the future.

I remember hanging my head but with a genuine smile on my face.

This is another example of where I would humbly submit that listening to podcasts has changed my life. It is not the case that I listened to someone who told me something I didn't know and that I decided to change how I live. Rather, listening to many varied, often quite philosophically deep discussions helped me crystallise thoughts, beliefs and, most concretely, life-principles which I had been internally chewing over for decades. Even since my teens.

Questions of what it means to be a wealthy person, as opposed to rich.

Why we do what we do. Why we don't do what we don't do.

Etcetera, etcetera.

If I may, a couple of favourite quotes:

It is better not to want something than to have it – Naval Ravikant

I love that one. I think about the person who lusts after a Ferrari and then finally scoops together enough moulah to buy one. Then he has to insure it, worry about passers-by scratching it, depreciation, where to keep it, where to drive it, where not to drive it, and so on.

I simply don't want one. Easy. Shitloads easier. Apply that approach to as many possessions as possible and you're immediately way better off.

Trade money for time, not time for money. You're going to run out of time first.

He is good, Naval. You should listen to him! But I imagined myself on my deathbed. Would it be more likely that I lay there, wheezing, wishing I had worked for another three years in the same job in the same home and become a bit richer...or being grateful that we had taken control, moved the Boys to a happy, rural community where they could make permanent friendships. Sadly, this is not an option for too many. But it is for a lot.

Back in the SAR

Decision to transition to Queensland, Australia, officially made.

However, after returning to our Asian island we soon realised that it would be wise to wait. The pandemic-omime raged in mid-"it's behind you"-performance. Friends and colleagues had dutifully made the trip to the UK, undergone the quarantine and then found themselves locked indoors for the remainder of their holiday until it was time to fly back to Hong Kong. The random nature of what type of restriction would be implemented where and for how long turned any island exit into a game of chance.

Like a futuristic video game, barriers were emerging, morphing and disappearing at borders across the World. With the abject lack of rationale, it was impossible to forecast what bureaucratic assault course would be imposed in front of us where and when.

So, we decided to have a final "goodbye" Christmas. This was in the summer of 2020.

I tentatively floated the idea that, well, if we were going to hang around until January, then we might as well crawl over the line for my next bonus payment date, the end of March.

Weeeeell, in that case, it makes sense to see out the full school year for the kids. Good point. And that leads us straight into summer (2021) which would be the perfect time to launch into a European "World Detour"! We toyed with the idea of road-tripping around the States, then Europe for six months. This sounded to Kate and me like a wonderfully imaginative (wannabe counter-cultural) display of our open-mindedness. Wouldn't it be terrific for the Boys!

At the same time the Hong Kong Special Administrative Region ("SAR") was undergoing some radical and rapid changes. As the rest of the World foolishly fretted over a false fear, China was steadily tightening its grip on the region. On the 30 June 2020, the NSL was passed in Hong Kong. It was written with intentional ambiguity. But it essentially scythed across existing law.

As a result of the NSL, if you had a lawsuit against a company for whatever infringement you were seeking to demonstrate in a court of law, the previous legal analysis of your case could be rendered irrelevant if you had posited something on- or off-line to which the powers-that-be took exception.

I spoke to lawyer friends and expats, some of whom had been in the SAR for 27 years, and they confirmed that this was effectively the end of One Country Two Systems.

Other friends, especially long time Hong Kongers, refused to recognise the changes as being such a big deal. Often, they would proffer painfully contorted comparisons to Western examples of similar rules but, taking a step back, it seemed clear to Kate and me that the Hong Kong we had so loved for six years was ebbing away.

A banker at BNP Paribas had to resign as a result of something he posted on Facebook. Independent media was being targeted and shut down. Schools were being required to sing the Chinese national anthem and support teachings on "Xi Jinping thought".

Of course, there was part of us that wanted to believe that the NSL was worse than it really was, as it would make our decision to jettison the lovely life we had built for ourselves that much easier.

But, in retrospect, I think we were right to see it for what it was.

Hong Kong Swan Song

We made the most out of our last 12 months in Hong Kong. I had returned at the beginning of June so that I could work remotely from our spare room in Hong Kong rather than our Sunshine Coast office in Montville. WFH would regularly consist of reading a book whilst comfortably reclined on the sofa with the laptop screen open and facing my left ear. Thus ensuring that I was "online".

Don't tell me I was the only one working from home from the sofa!

Indeed, colleagues in the UK with the luxury of a garden were busily building their man-sheds complete with beer fridge, flat screen TV and the latest sound system. One of my senior, countrified colleagues admitted to shooting a squirrel from his desk after he muted a conference call.

Kate and the Boys came back a month later. Contrary to our imagined fears, the Boys were fine with two weeks of quarantine in our apartment. For some reason they completely accepted and abided by the strict rule not to leave the apartment or its outside space and didn't test those particular boundaries once over the two weeks.

In stark contrast, as soon as the two weeks were over, they were running riot again and ignoring all parent-generated restrictions!

Anyway, we settled back in. I would say into a routine but, as with everywhere else where midwits were trying to legislate against an airborne virus, rules came in, were changed, disappeared, reappeared and so on.

Sometimes we were allowed to go to the Hong Kong Cricket Club, sometimes only until 6pm and other times not at all. The outdoor pool was closed, then opened, then closed again and then finally limited to 27 people. Someone had deemed the solution to be to surround the pool with aesthetically hideous plastic traffic barriers to ensure that, if you were to exit the pool, you had to run around the barriers to a guarded entry point and queue to get back in again.

Son: "But…but Daddy, why…".

Me: "Son…seriously, please…forget it…just...no reason!".

Particularly irksome was the mask mandate, which was imposed everywhere at all times, including outside. At one point, even on the isolated, wind-swept and sun-blazed peaks of the national parks. Despite being staunchly of the view that this was all utter bollocks, I did comply and justified it with the "when in Rome" mantra. In addition, I didn't expect to be allowed to piece together a winning argument in the face of an inevitably furious and yappy Cantonese onslaught.

Nevertheless, Hong Kong was still one of the better places to be at that time, as we frequently congratulated ourselves. Looking around the globe, speaking to expat friends about their home countries and also in my job daily to colleagues across the Asia Pacific region, the Hong Kong government allowed a greater degree of freedom than most of the developed World. We were never locked in our own homes and were always able to meet with friends in private venues.

I would call home to hear about how my beloved mother, in her 80s, was policed from stopping for a rest on a park bench as part of her regular walk. My dear sister was juggling working from home, home-schooling two young children and not finding that conducive to family dynamics.

I had to be careful in expressing my increasingly firm views on the whole abominable debacle. I was certain from March 2020 that this lockdown nonsense would generate far greater problems than the disease. That was in relation to the first order impacts even before one started to account for second order effects, such as the lack of trade and tourism into Africa, Asia and poorer countries in general. Those closest to the margin of being able to feed, house and educate themselves were going to suffer the greatest medium- and long-term pain.

However, I sensed in both my mother and my sister an element of buy-in for the maliciously manipulative mantra of benevolent compliance. Whereas, I considered myself to have a clear line of sight on how the government and MSM were talking shite, there is in all of us the wish to be well thought of. The government and media were loud-hailering in unison that compliance with these totalitarian edicts was the only way to save lives and those questioning the rules were essentially complicit in murder.

Such is the power of these institutions. Their misuse of that power made the truth sound evil. My honest assessment of the trade-off between harms and benefits made me sound like a callous psychopath.

However, life in Hong Kong carried on with, at its core, a portfolio of activities that were unaffected by dumb decrees. We were able to congregate at each other's houses for dinner and drinks and to enjoy hikes in the greenery.

In terms of the general mental well-being of the population, I can only observe that the expats, when comparing to their home countries, were sanguine about the rules in place in Hong Kong. The issue that kept coming up was that of trips home to see family. It was broadly agreed that you were risking permanent family scarring by booking yourselves in for three weeks of hotel quarantine (Hong Kong's requirement) with young children and a working parent.

But people did manage.

Of my native Hong Konger friends and colleagues, some were more focussed on the NSL and I was surprised at how many were talking about emigrating, mostly to the UK. Others (my interpretation) were drawn into the Hong Kong groupthink on COVID. One of my colleagues had had a young son right at the beginning of the plandemic and was genuinely too concerned to take him out of the flat for over half a year. It was tongue in cheek (or was it) when he joked that he would place him on the windowsill in his apartment at the right time of day so as to catch some moments of sunshine. As time went on, he relaxed very slightly but it was gradual to say the least.

Another colleague had recently married and was working through health issues with a view to having a family. They did not want to take the "vaccine" but saw it as inevitable given attitudes in their social circle. When I asked if they wanted to see some of the statistics on potential side effects, they said that they would rather not know.

A reasoned decision to ignore information that might cause an awkward family confrontation. This is the power of consensus narrative…of groupthink. Some people do not even want to be shown the competing view.

At this stage in my work mindset, I had utterly given up on tempering my views for the sake of fitting in with the hive mind. It was an extraordinary performance to witness colleague after colleague take the jab in Hong Kong, to then be unusually bed-ridden – not able to get up and walk around - for two or three days and then talk about it as a badge of honour.

These were highly educated people with access to international news, statistics and balancing views. And yet they managed to tell themselves that this was normal, that it showed that the "vaccines" were working. They would refer to the effects of the flu vaccines but loftily ignore the fact that no-one was ever bedridden by them.

The greater the harm the injection had perpetrated on their health, the greater the victim perceived their sacrifice to the greater social good.

Fuck. Me.

I searched for like-minded sceptics, but they were few and far between. The closest I could find were those who respected my right to choose.

The bank offered employees two days' extra holiday for taking the "vaccine". Recovery time. Or a bribe. To take experimental gene therapy. Seriously.

Of course, there were some that had been unable to withstand the deluge of scaremongering and were genuinely spooked by the danger posed by the virus. However, it was the combination of lust to be back on a plane and the pervasive group coercion that drove them to acquiesce to the clot shot.

Many expats had not seen their families for over 18-24 months and anything that would facilitate a trip home together with the warm momentum of a growing consensus was something they would eagerly accept.

But it also should not be overlooked that, for a lot of the bankers where I worked, the ease and regularity with which they travelled, popping into the Cathay lounge as they wheeled through airports, was a fundamental cornerstone of their self-worth. Zipping from country to country for a pitch, a conference or a series of marketing meetings was third party evidence of the intellectual property uniquely contained in their cranium. Why else would your company cough up the time and money it took to put you on a flight for hours at a time, watching movies with Shiraz-tinged teeth, to meet with people whose own business trips were justified by the fact that you had just visited them?!

Such was the mutual back-scratchy nature of unnecessary business travel in Asia. I once flew from Hong Kong to Singapore (3 hours 45 mins – two movies) and back in a day for a deal-celebrating lunch.

Some team leaders (pre-COVID) would fly somewhere every week without their team or boss even knowing where or why.

Working from home obliterated this predictably fragile illusion of in-person value. The longer that individuals were asked to perform from the low-cost, time-efficient confines of their own apartment the more obvious it would be that business travel would never revert to the vulgar levels previously attained.

However, the sooner that executives got back on planes the further away from flat zero that slide would have been allowed to reach.

My UK colleague with whom I would have enormously loud and enjoyable office debates was utterly frank about taking the jibby-jab in Hong Kong. He saw it as inevitable for him to be able to holiday in the near future, thought the queue for injections would be shorter in Hong Kong and so decided to just get it over and done with.

The disappointing irony for him was that, although it was the Pfizer jab, when he returned to the UK at the end of his secondment to Hong Kong, it was not recognised by the powers-that-be in the UK as it had not been administered by the NHS. He would have to be needled four times to be deemed "vaccinated" and that was before boosters.

Such is the calm, rational logic underpinning the "vaccine" strategy.

Penny Bayhem

The mood in Hong Kong did degenerate as time passed. An increasing number of rules were introduced that simply did not make sense, leading to a groundswell of frustration. However, what really set the expat community aflutter was the Hong Kong approach to test and trace which culminated, at least in our time, with Penny Bay.

Penny Bay was a built-for-purpose COVID containment camp. Cases were so low in Hong Kong that it was deemed possible to isolate those who had been in contact with a positive case. And then to put them in an isolation camp for two weeks.

Job done!

These were not positive cases. But rather those that had been in contact with a positive case.

Anyone that was positive, whether ill or not, was secured in a special hospital facility (this is true).

A resplendent illustration of the madness was that of a gym-goer who subsequently tested positive. Everyone who had been to the gym at a time that coincided with his work out was sent to Penny Bay for a fortnight. Everyone with whom he had played rugby was sent to Penny Bay. Everyone whom he had played rugby against was sent to Penny Bay. For a fortnight.

He, having in truth tested positive, was sent to hospital where he was attended to (by all accounts in a freezing cold, ice-white ward) by hazmat-suited medical staff whilst having to while away the hours purely with his imagination (a la The Shining).

Those of us on the rugby WhatsApp group were then treated to a series of videos from within the bowels of Penny Bay. Sparse, prison-like rooms presented the unenviable challenge of a bleak two weeks of isolation on jail rations.

This story became common knowledge and most families, including ours, put together an emergency bag - in case they were collared - containing books, an iPad with downloaded movies, spicy sauces and camouflaged alcohol (bottles of coke laced with vodka).

Another tale did the rounds of a mother whose six-month old child tested positive whilst she did not and so the two were separated.

These true events did the job they were presumably intended to, creating an informal self-policing of friend groups. I was monstrously disappointed to see the rugby boys shout down any hesitation to get "vaccinated" from those who dared voice concerns. Rugby games were open only to the vaxxed: when putting forward your name on the WhatsApp group a little needle emoji was used to confirm your status. Rugby socials were only for the compliant.

Yes, the rugby team had been the most badly hit by the early Penny Bay incident. But at the same time, Kate's netball teams were able to operate a more open, informed consent approach. Live and let live. That, despite the visceral tale of mother and child being ruthlessly separated.

Oh – and I should mention: the gym-goer, the one who tested positive and was taken into medical custody, promptly tested negative a couple of days later and was summarily released. Whilst his rugby teammates had to see out their full 14-day stretches!

In retrospect, I would argue that the initial Penny Bay episode (there were plenty more) was a morale-poisoning moment. Friends started to worry about the quantity and location of venues where potential guests may have mixed. Families wanted to narrow their list of contacts. And contacts' contacts. Minimise the risk of being Penny Bay-ed.

Kate and I had already decided we were leaving and everything we saw around us seemed to justify that decision.

Trough Job

My job. I liked it. It was interesting...different day to day, every day. It was pressured. However, I had managed to de-stress it by working out what my worst-case scenario career was (being fired?) and becoming comfortable with that (I can remember a friend's look of horror as I set out this seemingly ambition-free analysis).

My job spanned Asia Pacific but with on-going connections to the rest of the World. It involved real objects and projects: planes, trains and automobiles...railways, hospitals, roads. A large proportion of it was centred on energy and my bank was one of the most skilled proponents of financing renewable energy but also oil and liquefied natural gas. There was plenty of scope for me to green-splain if I so wished.

I had worked long and competently enough to be in a management position. This, combined with a diligent and very capable team, meant that I was able to minimise my volume of roll-up-your-sleeves, detailed work and was able to tick over by managing the bigger picture.

Quite honestly, my team members were better than me and I was able to ride on their coattails whilst doing what I enjoyed, following the daily economic and political news across the varied patchwork of jurisdictions in the region.

The pay was more than decent, especially at a 15% tax rate, although the nature of Hong Kong was that it was almost impossible not to give up the majority of that tax advantage through living and schooling costs.

Essentially, it had become a comfortable job that was well paid and that also held a certain amount of prestige.

However, there were elements of it that I found increasingly difficult to live with:

1) Divorced from reality

This is a a bug bear of mine: my doomsayer argument that the World never properly paid the price for the Global Financial Crisis ("GFC"). Through a combination of disastrously unethical policy choices, central banks have robbed a generation of hard-working savers and boosted the coffers of the already unnecessarily rich.

Most people will know that, since 2009, asset bubbles have been pumped through a combination of insanely low interests and quantitative easing.

However, the sheer scale of misallocation of resources was atrocious to me. The mispricing of risk, the fire-hosing of financial liquidity at risky projects rendered the intellectual aspect of my role ever less relevant. There was no point saying, "this makes no sense" as we had been saying that for years. Impossible loans were made at blatantly inappropriate pricing levels.

Now, many would argue that there is a case to be made for lending tens of millions of dollars to a renewable project that would not otherwise get off the ground. However, what I saw was equity investors taking those loans and immediately de-risking themselves to run off with a large, government-backed profit, for the project then to struggle and suck in rescue money.

This feeds into a far, far larger question about our current financial system and where we really are today.

My view sounds extreme, but I hear a lot of very deep financial thinkers who are of a similar disposition. Here goes:

Ever since the USD and, by extension, the rest of the World left the gold standard in 1971 it was inevitable that governments would exploit that lack of an anchor to their now fiat currencies. Indeed, governments have since promised to spend more of their taxpayers' money than they bring in (via taxes) in order to win votes with give-away policies.

This increase of expense over income has been funded by increased national debt both recorded officially on- (normally seen as a percentage of Gross Domestic Product ("GDP")) and off-balance sheet (pensions, benefits and other entitlements).

In a competitive environment the price of the debt (interest cost) would adjust upwards and discipline would be applied by the market as to what levels of debt could be sustained. These market forces are prevented from applying by central banks which set borrowing rates at levels that suit political agendas. These interest rates are essentially the price of money (*The Price of Time* according to *Edward Chancellor*): central to every market interaction we undertake. Having mispriced the debt via fiat, the central banks are then able to ensure it is still purchased through a combination of money-printing and securities regulations (for example requiring pension funds to hold a certain proportion of that debt).

In short, the fiat system is designed to allow governments to buy votes from taxpayers (paid with taxpayers own *goddam* money) up to the point when it becomes so blatantly unsustainable that enough of the markets call bullshit. Or a sufficient portion of the markets, so that that the central banks and their co-conspirators lose control.

In my view, this time is upon us and may form part of the explanation for the otherwise inexplicable actions that we are seeing being taken around the World. Just for fun (from usdebtclock.org):

USD (on balance sheet) debt:	over	USD 31,000,000,000,000
Per US taxpayer that is:	over	USD 248,000 per person

Off balance sheet debt is estimated to at least triple those numbers.

In short, the US is bust and so is the World. There needs to be a debt reset.

That may well be what is happening right now – an unfairly lop-sided debt jubilee. The problem is that the vast majority of creditors (those owed the money) are those expecting pensions and other entitlements. Defaulting on those will cause extreme poverty where it was least expected and had been assumed to have been eradicated – destructive civilian unrest would be almost inevitable.

I suspect we will see the current geopolitical and financial (and social) crisis crescendo to the point where enough citizens are pleading for a solution that a debt restructuring into a Central Bank Digital Currency ("CBDC") will be welcomed by the tortured masses. Maybe the quid pro quo will be Universal Basic Income ("UBI"). It will be called something ingeniously euphemistic, but it will be a debt jubilee / restructuring – a default.

As an interesting aside, another wonderful example of the wisdom of the ancients that we somehow strove to wipe from our memories, is that of debt jubilees.

In Sumerian / Babylonian times it was a feature of their financial system to have a debt jubilee every 50 years. This meant that all debts were wiped away every 50 years. The ancients had developed this as a method to control what they knew would happen otherwise, being spiralling levels of debt to the point of unsustainability (per now). This knowledge that all debts would be wiped clean meant that either the lenders managed their loans down to zero as the jubilee date approached or the borrowers were able to provide sufficient assurance, security or collateral to the lender to occasion sufficient confidence in both parties that the debt would be re-issued immediately after the passing of the jubilee.

A jubilee would be controlled by design and made known to all well in advance.

I fear what we are going to see is more of a calamitous, chaotic global default. And I don't really want to be shuffling my snout through the corporate trough when that happens.

2) Green-mania

I have unpopular views on global warming. I suspect that in penning these mini-memoirs I will disenfranchise a huge proportion of any audience I might have garnered and that the following will see to a big chunk of that. But, hey, I have to be honest:

- I question whether and how much the climate is warming;
- I question where it is warming and where it isn't;
- I question whether warming is a bad thing (as opposed to cooling);
- I question why the IPCC's baseline "pre-industrial temperature" being the average of those temperatures that were measured between 1850-1900 is the correct baseline;
- I question why people think the IPCC is independent when its existence is dependent on it finding the problem that it finds;
- I question why we focus on CO2 when I think there are far more harmful and genuine pollutants;
- I question how many people in the developing World our policies - which inevitably lead to increased energy costs - will affect…and just how badly;

- I question the ARROGANCE that we have the capacity to control the World's temperature in 80 years' time to 1.5 degrees or not by dialling up and down human CO2 emissions?!?!
- And don't get me started on computer modelling. Trying to mathematise planet Earth's climate? What utter self-indulgent horseshit that is!

In summary, I do not think the science is settled. Not that I acknowledge "settled science" as a valid concept. It should go without saying that there is an existing scientific body of knowledge that *must* be constantly challenged. Science is the process of that challenge. Science is – almost literally – not believing the experts!

Using less, using wisely, being cleaner and behaving with proper respect to our beautiful planet should be a given for all of us. And these concepts should be presented as part of all of our children's enlightened education.

Distributed solar has obvious benefits in places such as Africa, India and Australia. Nuclear has been regulated out of economic reality by activists and this should be reversed. But running around the World frantically slamming in wind and solar farms with trillions of taxpayers' money as we can see projects around the globe underperform dramatically is to intentionally screw the planet and its inhabitants. Certainly, it will endanger vast swathes of the poor.

Anyway, as you might have guessed, I had a lot of questions about the Environmental, Social and Governance ("ESG") policies that I was seeing enforced by my bank. In my short time in my latest senior role, the bank went from financing projects at a decent price where something very unexpected would have to go wrong for the loan to not be repaid, to under-pricing projects where you would hope you had left the bank by the time the project did go wrong.

The bank rolled out a series of online training pogroms – these are direct quotes that I noted at the time:

"The Group's CSR [Corporate Social Responsibility] ambition must be supported personally by all Group employees."

"This system must be part of the DNA of each employee, in [country of bank's incorporation] and abroad."

How did we get to the point where a global bank was telling its employees what they "must" think – personally – on an issue such as climate change.

The ESG drumbeat was becoming incessant. Every day, we would have to call in to a conference presentation about a deal that had some contrived ESG angle to it and listen for an hour. These were invariably painfully self-congratulatory. We talked about making anything and everything a "green" loan or a "sustainability-linked" loan. These were loans that would have been made in any case. However, we were encouraged to excavate and polish some pre-existing feature to then amplify and rebrand as virtuous.

Highly intelligent, over-educated people would drone on like automatons parroting Sustainable Development Goals (DON'T…!) without questioning anything. A specialist green team bloomed from zero to four over a year. A team that seriously added nothing but green garnish. Sanctimonious parsley.

We talked about a "blue" (water usage friendly) loan for a Chinese steel manufacturer, for the love of God!

It was strange. Genuinely freaky. It is self-evident that in Asia, efficiently-sourced energy is a fundamental, path-critical and absolute necessity for these countries to be able to feed their populations, stave off civil unrest and survive in the battle for resources. I was working with colleagues who had worked in the energy industry for 30 plus years and for whom the underlying politics and human needs were an ever-present given.

Yet they chose – yes, chose – to ignore their own first-hand experience and knowledge. In order to serve a top-down, politically motivated end.

That bedrock of understanding was in each and every one of them. Yet to keep their career on the right tracks they would obsequiously repudiate what they knew to be true.

Yet I was the one seen to be ethically questionable.

The ESG push through the financial system is an ingeniously well-scripted psychological offering that panders to financiers' lust for monetary wealth whilst cloaking these riches in the perceived robes of virtue.

Individuals are simultaneously able to accumulate both dollar and do-gooder credits.

To access this societally-blessed treasure all that is required was not so much cognitive dissonance as wilful cognitive dismissal.

Virtue-bolstered riches were always going to win the day.

Yet we were watching the roll-out of renewables strain the sound banking model in real time. Many a morning's work would splutter into exasperated swapping of nonsensical developments - bafflement as yet another wind turbine collapsed through the seabed, the weight of snow smashed solar panels and buckled stanchions, critical electrical connections were overloaded, parts further delayed, over-committed suppliers bankrupted, etc, etc.

Don't get me wrong. I absolutely love the idea of cheap, reliable and clean energy. But I fear that wind and solar renewable energy meet these criteria only in narrow circumstances and for the Western World to somehow unilaterally decide that it is a broad solution to our energy needs is palpable madness. And it will not end well.

3) Diversity, Inclusion and Equity ("DIE")

Urgh. Oh dear, oh dear. Where do I start? We didn't keep a close enough eye on these people. Their ideas were just too off the wall to pay serious attention to them.

In fact, even today, the overwhelming majority of people agree that this woke cancer is nonsense and we cannot believe grown-ups are taking it seriously.

Yet it's everywhere. This insane encouragement to include pronouns in your mini biography. Discussions about babies being racist. Eight-year-olds being able to consent to puberty blockers, even castration.

We didn't take the woke fundamentalists' pie-eyed, piss-stupid, pious protestations seriously enough as they started insisting on their bizarre, cultish ideology. We should have stamped on the Owen Jones-lauding midwits farting forth from Blair-contrived "university" courses at fourth rate ex-polytechnics when we had the chance.

But the heads you win, tails you lose arguments that they promoted have metastasised and the effects of the disease are entrenched. Their relativist, ego-centric ("my lived experience") constructs are designed to be impenetrable to the majority and circular to those questioning in good faith. Either way, you're a racist, sexist capitalist.

Having been robbed of the ability to think for themselves by a schooling system that demands the exact opposite, the intellectually flimsy that dominate mid-management positions allowed these poisons to take root. And now we have to navigate DIE-hard woke cultists everywhere: schools, all levels of government, HR functions, para-legal positions… and even senior management.

Even in Hong Kong.

I mean what a load of pernicious bollocks.

I pushed back. I was being asked, as one of my objectives for the year, to proactively seek to balance my team of seven 50:50 male:female.

Having taken a principled approach to hiring for my team based on ability, personality, experience, etc, I was now being formally instructed to make hiring decisions taking into account the nature of a candidate's genitalia.

Now, if you think the game is rigged from a sexism point of view, fair enough. But that is illegal for a European bank and it should be contested on that point of law and called out wherever it is found. 100%.

But what you really, REALLY shouldn't do is artificially force the outcome.

First and foremost, how desperately, insultingly condescending. I have worked with a multitude of women throughout my career and they have been just as competent as the men. I don't want to make a distinction but maybe women stand out on average as being more diligent. Maybe more risk averse…which can be a good or a bad thing…depending on the thing!

I also flatly reject this under-contested false assumption that any divergence from a 50:50 outcome is somehow proof of an inherent bias. I haven't seen the same argument being made for binmen or deep-sea divers…or builders or gardeners or cage-fighters…or nurses or teachers or florists.

I am sorry, but men and women, on an aggregate macro level, differ. In a number of ways. It therefore stands to reason that they will, at a macro level, self-select for different careers. It's a genuinely cynical implication that, if we don't have half the Managing Directors and Directors over 40 years age split 50:50 then there is something nefarious afoot.

The idea that, if we don't have those valuing corporate prestige and money over family time evenly balanced across male and female, then someone is intentionally hiring in a discriminatory fashion.

If mothers, who grew their babies inside their wombs for nine months ahead of giving excruciating birth whilst still attached to their beloved offspring before then nurturing them with their very own supremely unique breastmilk…if those mothers don't make the same work/life, cash/care decisions then this is somehow unchallengeable evidence that an entrenched, chauvinist bigot prioritised boyish sports chat over his team's performance.

We are allowing there to be a dominant view in society that decrees, if the sexes don't equally value and achieve bullshit jobs, then we will force the issue by making it so.

Well, I refused (the objective) and I am proud of that. My next hire happened to be female, by the way. Because she was the best for the job.

On the woke accusations on racism, this vile, indulgent decadence also becomes laughable in Asia. Whilst the West gaily has a nervous breakdown fretting about how racist we are, Asia Pacific delivers to the World a consummate masterclass in racism. Whilst vacuous idiots are wasting their time on this planet whining about white privilege, the Chinese will happily tell you that they benefit from Han privilege because…well…because they are genetically superior.

Indonesians benefit from Indonesian privilege, Singaporeans from Singaporean privilege…you don't get too many non-Filipina politicians in the Philippines. And in Malaysia they still have racial apartheid. Yes, they have a different legal system depending on whether you are racially Bumiputera or not.

Some posit that the Middle East is even worse.

Why don't we just call it majority privilege and get on with life, huh?

When I was growing up it was important to recognise that you were privileged (economically, not racially) and the overpowering message was not to waste that privilege. That fundamentally includes consideration of and supporting the less well off. And that is the message I will be teaching my children.

Not this woke gobble-dee-gook which only the supremely irritating, angry and inadequate 5% spend their wasted lives screeching about.

At my bank, we even started having Women's Days when we are encouraged to wear purple clothes to recognise the achievements and importance of women. Like...we don't recognise the importance of the mothers of our children FOR FUCK'S SAKES!!

There you go. Three reasons why I was ready to leave my job. You could add to that, the emerging creep of China into Hong Kong.

However, the main factor was the pull of being able to bring up the Boys in a green, rural, community environment surrounded by outdoor living, sports and kindness. That was the number one reason it was time to make the change and leave.

But I did also feel I had run out of room in believing in my day-to-day job for the reasons above.

Hexit Kexit-Jobexit

Again, I don't want to go into painful detail but, having spent over two decades with the bank and having left behind a trail of bullet-proof transactions, inspired juniors and demonstrated that success could be married to kind ethics, I had hoped for a mutually beneficial departure.

However, my boss ignored my request for voluntary redundancy, kicked back my request for a nine-month sabbatical (as had been agreed in writing with HR) and presented me with an ultimatum to choose between either:

a) Resign; or
b) Take three months leave of absence and promise to return.

I asked if a) would include me retaining my deferred bonuses (the vast majority of bonuses were spread out over a three-year period post earning them). He said he had not thought of this and that he would get back to me.

When I was eventually presented with my "Separation Agreement" I thought it only wise to invest the time and money to have an employment lawyer take a cursory look through it. She told me she had never seen such a skewed contract for an individual that was leaving via mutual agreement.

So, I went for option b) but without ever meaning to keep the promise. Option b) meant that I would be paid for those three months and that, if I could bridge an extra two weeks after the three-month period, I would scoop up deferred bonuses relating to three previous years.

I justified this deceit in my mind by telling myself that my boss had manufactured this insidious binary option in utterly bad faith (he immediately reverted to the language of the bank versus me) and that he was quite literally paying me to lie to him. Idiot.

But I hated lying to my team. I mean, when their boss goes off-line for three months and leaves Hong Kong with the monumental COVID hurdles to surmount on the way back, there was naturally a strong suspicion in their minds that I might not return.

But I could not be honest with them.

In particular, I remember the team PA – a supremely wise Hong Kong lady who had been with the bank for over a quarter of a century – looking deep into my eyes, over the leaving lunch I was hosting, and asking me if I was coming back.

Along with some fragments of the Peking duck upon which we were gorging, I think I blurted out something along the lines of, "absolutely, that's the plan". Consoling myself that somehow that "plan" proviso was sufficient a message.

That still makes me sad.

Flatexit and Leaving Thinks

After nearly six happy years living in our flat, packing up and moving out was never going to be fun. Crikey, we had accumulated a volume of crap. And so we culled. We donated, we sold, we gave away and we threw away.

At the time, it felt as if we had cut to the core. However, we still managed to chalk up over 200 boxes that were ruthlessly packed up and taken away before our eyes. We said our happy-sad goodbyes to what had been our home.

My leaving drinks / evening turned into a disastrous experience, which I will always remember / not remember.

A group of us had arranged for an evening of early beers starting in central Hong Kong. Originally, the plan had been to execute a rollocking pub crawl from Central through some favourite haunts, ending in my local pub, The Smugglers, which was likely to allow curb-side drinking past the official 10pm corona-curfew.

Rather predictably, with a group of strong, diverse characters, the evening was a little hijacked. We ended up over-ordering piles of meat in the steak restaurant nearest to the pub in which we had started and stayed. I remember fielding a grilling from a Parliamentary Committee panel across the table of mostly jokey abuse about being an anti-vaxxer. At the same time I was being force-fed a dizzying barrage of sambuca and tequila shots (do boys ever grow up?).

My memory gently mists away as I look back on the evening sliding hazily past 10pm, although I do remember the taxi to Wan Chai where a number of bars were known to take a less forensic approach to vax passports.

I still had my bag from work and my sober-daytime wallet. I had not adopted my night-out battle gear, as one would normally do when entering the notorious night-time nether zone of "The Wanch".

From the point of arrival onwards, the memory snapshots become blurrier, more abstract and then stop altogether.

And then I woke up on the Saturday morning.

With no memory. Not a 100% unique experience, truth be told. Although, this loss of memory felt more…absolute…complete.

Anyway, I didn't even sleep in that much and was able to function close enough to normal to avoid significant rebuke from Kate.

It was only three full days after that I discovered what had really happened. I was at work when I logged on to my HSBC bank account.

The feeling that I experienced (a softer version of which I am now sensing, just retelling the story) when I clocked two ATM cash withdrawals from my current account on the Friday night/ Saturday morning totalling HKD 70,000 (USD 10,000) is one of a galling yearn to be able to replay events differently.

A ball of leaden self-loathing grew deep in my gut. An evil from which you want to avert your eyes and just hope it goes away.

What the hell happened?!

Well, I kind of knew…feared that I already knew the answer. Only two weeks prior, a colleague of mine had told me how his physical trainer had been drugged at last orders, as the bar staff were clearing him out. The drug allowed his assailants to march him to a cash point where he willingly either gave them his PIN or took out the money himself to then hand over. He was robbed of a similar amount. The drug was scopolamine (also known and The Devil's Breath). It has been used in the past as a truth serum drug and is known to wipe the victim's memory whilst at the same time making them unnaturally compliant and truth-telling. Scopolamine is also a legal drug used to combat motion sickness. Apparently, due to the reduced opportunities for cross-border drug trafficking visited by the COVID border restrictions, there had been a significant emergence of this type of theft in Hong Kong.

I was another victim.

Upon logging on and seeing this documented evidence as proof of my own victimhood and having tried to gather my composure, I marched to my nearest HSBC branch to report the crime. I am both a thoroughly hopeless liar and someone who would torment myself with guilt and fear if I tried to cover up such an incident. So, I messaged Kate from the queue at the bank.

HSBC was simply not interested. File a police report and then we will look at it, they said.

I played out an imagined conversation with the police:

- What happened?
    - o Dunno
- Who, how many, what did they look like?
    - o Dunno, dunno, dunno
- Where, what time?
    - o Dunno, dunno

Maybe they could check the ATMs to see if they had cameras? But even then, as I understood it, there would be no crime. Even if the video showed the perpetrators keying in the PIN (it could have been me tapping it in) it would have appeared voluntary.

Maybe I was making an excuse, as I just wanted not to have to think about it. But it did also occur to me that I had been out, outside of curfew and in bars that I should not have entered, given my vax-free state. My family and I were due to leave in two weeks. Could a COVID infringement (or four) hamper that? I would need police clearance for my Australian visa.

I decided to leave it. Take the hit. Financial and emotional. The fuckers.

I didn't sleep properly for a number of weeks after that. That leaden globe would barge through the merest moments of lighter sleep and assert itself with the unbounded expanse of imagination that the darkness provides.

In a fortuitously timed Dark Horse podcast, I greedily clutched the message that when we make mistakes, we need to analyse, assess and dwell on them. Berate ourselves, absolutely. But only up to the point when that self-recrimination has worked its benefit. Rebuke, reproach, reprimand but once that self-admonishment has done its job in ensuring that no such mistake will be made again, move on. Torturing oneself beyond this point is self-destructive and a net-negative.

Anyway. That was a bit shit. And it did overshadow our last weeks in Hong Kong. At the same time, it made me want to draw a line, depart and move on!

Interesting aside: having previously never heard of it, I then discovered that scopolamine is mentioned by Aldous Huxley in his epilogue to Brave New World where he cites it as potentially the real-World drug closest to the soma of his book - the feel-good drug that he warned about in a World where humans are willingly suppressed.

Oogah!

For a whole range of reasons, our family was more than ready to leave Hong Kong. But we were leaving behind experiences we will keep with us forever...even more so friendships and the phenomenal new perspectives they brought with them.

When you first arrive in Hong Kong, there is a cliché amongst the expats that you spend the first year trying to make friends and the rest of your time there trying to lose most of them.

That's unfair. We made some amazing connections. The Hong Kong expat community is a wonderful combination of nationalities from all over the World: Scandinavians to Southern Europeans, Americans to Japanese, Indians to South Africans. It is true that nearly all the expats are there for the purposes of their work and, given that placements are temporary (mine was only slated to be three years initially), many friendships are necessarily transitory.

However, we were lucky to have made friends that I know will last. Whilst not wanting to sound wanky, the calibre of discussion was always fantastic. Maybe it was being away from one's home patch, maybe it was a dose of reality by living on the doorstep of China, maybe it was seeing with one's own eyes how politics and culture interacted across the region, but conversations were significantly more honest and fearless than those I had comfortably circled around in Battersea.

Or maybe it was just that I was hearing different perspectives...at last.

One of our deeply beloved friend activities was to meet with our charismatic Russian friends on a Sunday evening. Just a five-minute walk from our front door there was an over-priced, pizza-serving beach bar hosted by an endearingly eccentric Hong Konger, Alfa. If you were unlucky, the perma-sloshed Italian owner would also be lingering close to the till, desperate to mumble his incoherent life story to anyone not firm enough to walk away.

We would meet there with our respective boys, armed with a bottle each of either bubbles, rosé or intriguing white wine.

Once the $45 (equivalent) pizzas had been delivered, we would shuffle and clink around the corner of the beach to where the South China Sea reassuringly clashed with the rocks.

We did not have a name for our Sunday evenings until our friends' son decided to strip off, beat his chest and shout, "Oogah…OOGAH!!".

We pissed ourselves in disbelief as Rex and Raf swiftly took up the challenge and followed suit.

A Lord of the Flies, viscerally natural boy moment.

Over time the lads would go on to build elaborately-imagined homes on the rocks out of driftwood, compete in spear fights and marvel at their bioluminescent footprints in the sand as the sun hazily slid down behind the South China Sea horizon.

At the same time, us parents would confidently march into conversational territory where few would dare to tread. What might be debilitating social landmines in most polite company were trampled on as we felt free to experiment with and crash test ideas that normally reside in heavily barb-wired No Man's (or Woman's) Land.

We loved it. We loved how the boys combined. We loved our friends. The beach, the wine, the view. How comfortable-yet-naughty our conversations were.

Those are the elements of Hong Kong we will miss the most.

PART II - EARLY TRANSITION
España

"Fill your life with experiences. Not things. Have stories to tell, not stuff to show."

Anonymous

Destination Spain

Having successfully been drugged and robbed, culled surplus clobber, crated a shipping container full of degradable cardboard boxes, vacated our home, deceived colleagues, sold the car, tearfully farewelled our friends and packed for a four-month World Detour, we were ready to depart Honkers Bonkers. Destination Spain.

But that was not what it felt like as we prepared to take off. At all. The background stress constantly sprayed perpetual white noise as a daily soundtrack to accompany our last weeks. In particular, there was still an awful lot of documentation to worry about. Each link in the intricate paperchain could potentially rip and leave us flapping. PCR tests for Kate and me, COVID locator forms, Spanish locator forms, Spanish health forms, Spanish tracking app, proof of accommodation etc.

None of the family was "vaccinated". The MSM was furiously hyping up the travel restrictions on the vaxxed, never mind the vax-free. Whilst we ensured that we were reading the ever-evolving requirements there was always going to be that spectre of doubt until we were physically in the air.

Maybe now is a good time to ask and answer the bleedingly obvious question: why did we not get "vaccinated" and, in declining to do so, make matters so much more difficult for ourselves? My thinking behind not getting the clot shot:

VacciNOlogic

From the outset, I took a deep interest in nearly every aspect of the plandemic.

As you have already read, a lot happened in the meantime. I made it out to Australia four weeks later and again over Easter/May, the latter visit after Australia had implemented its now (in)famous closed borders program.

Over those early months of February, March and April 2020 reliable information started to emanate, for example from Italy and the Diamond Princess. I had become increasingly confident of the view that the press coverage and policies of governments were grotesque over-reactions to what was a serious and occasionally deadly disease. Yes, this was a nasty virus that was unusually dangerous to the old and frail. However, the risk stratification was clear from a very early stage (more so on the question of age; the obesity risk became clearer later).

From afar, I remember the pride and hope I felt when the UK stood firm and said, this is a virus and it will do what viruses do. The senior public health officials made pragmatic statements consistent with the body of accumulated scientific knowledge.

And I remember the galling disappointment when the UK made a screeching handbrake turn and locked down. I knew immediately that it would be politically unviable to "unlock down" easily. I remember saying, Boris will not be able to lift this…if he does, he will be blamed for each and every death thereafter irrespective of the justification in that.

The economic damage. The effects on the poorest, not just in the UK but globally. These, in my view, were going to be cataclysmic. People forget that, at the end of 2019, we were already sucking our teeth and wondering how the financial system would withstand the mother of all recessions after an historic bull run driven by massive money printing. Trump had pump-primed the US economy with a view to buying his re-election and a lot of the lingering cancers from the Great Financial Crisis were beginning to metastasise in a forbidding form.

That was all BEFORE the 'Rona.

As April slid past and the data became ever more self-explanatory, I became ever more non-plussed. Boris had to lift all restrictions now, do a public, forgiveness-beseeching mea culpa and open up life as normal.

Surely. How else – through what other possible route – could you intelligently argue we get out of this?!

Answer: the "vaccines".

If we could develop and roll out new "vaccines" for COVID, then this would be, not only a justification for the unprecedented totalitarianism meted out on the public, but also for its continuation.

However, every source of education I could find on this question was withering:

- Scientists have been trying to develop a coronavirus vaccine for decades without success;
- The most optimistic, outlier expert I heard over that time was saying it would take at least 18 months (at that stage, people would have revolted at the idea of lockdowns over such an extended period);
- Long term safety data needs TIME...and humans have yet to find a way to bend time.

I did not hear one scientist suggest that producing, trialling and obtaining approval for a vaccine was even remotely realistic in the timescale required. Waiting for an effective vaccine was a scientific non-starter.

But over the course of the 2020 summer months, the messaging softened.

As the narrative gradually turned and it became increasingly clear that mRNA "vaccines" were the proposed ladders down which our political leaders would seek to clamber from their hideously unethical, unscientific and destructive lockdowns, I knew I was going to keep a close eye on how these innovations were going to be trialled and approved.

So, based on the above, it is totally fair to say that my starting point was sceptical...suspicious even. That is a bias I would be mad to ignore but to which I happily admit.

But then I would fervently argue, for me and my family, that it is my duty to be sceptical of brand-new gene therapy technology being developed at breakneck speed under biblical duress. My mantra in the office, when asked if I would take the "vaccine", was as follows:

- mRNA "vaccines" have never before been approved – this is new technology;
- no-one has ever managed to approve a vaccine for a coronavirus;
- Vaccines normally take around ten years to obtain their full approval;
- There simply cannot be an assessment of any long-term side effects; and, importantly
- I could not conceive of greater conflicts of interest than those pervading the "vaccine" roll out.

On this last point, I am not even focussing on the fact global pharmaceutical companies have raked in record-breaking tens of billions of profits through a product for which they carry no liability. That's quite a concern in and of itself.

When I reflect on the following words, I worry that they may not sound credible - my view that the conflicts of interest are so overwhelming that they made the Emergency Use Approvals ("EUAs") a foregone conclusion. However, I think the apparent hyperbole is completely justified.

Western governments had utilised emergency powers, designed for times of national threat, to commandeer the trust of their respective populations with a view to cancelling a number of their basic human rights. The justification, they proclaimed, was the scientific Greater Good. They had imposed devastation on their economics, spent billions on PPE and track & trace, shuttered hundreds of thousands of SMEs, over-ruled mental health, any other medical ailments, forbidden final kisses to loved ones, isolated the ably-challenged, etc, etc...for the scientific Greater Good.

Western governments had essentially said, en masse, make colossal emotional, physical, monetary, irreversible sacrifices and trust us. You need to do this and it is the right thing to do. Trust us.

These same governments then went all-in on "vaccines". Some of the pharma companies could not commit to pursuing this commercially uncertain course until the pre-orders justified the cost of development.

As a result, the governments pre-bought hundreds of billions of dollars' worth of "vaccines" that were under early stages of development and underpinned by unproven technology. On top of the trust they demanded by law (let's brush over that contradiction), the governments spent billions of taxpayers' money on what was, at that time, a speculative view that the experimental "vaccines" would be successful and safe... and approved.

That's quite a bet. The stake: monumental, population-wide personal sacrifices and suffering plus the gargantuan tax burden on our children... and our children's children.

Imagine if that bet had failed.

I don't think it's an exaggeration, a hyperbole, to say that the survival of Western government (and arguably the underlying societies themselves) rested on the successful development and approval of mRNA "vaccines".

And they were approved (under EUA). Eight of them worldwide (not all mRNA). Within a matter of months. From zero <u>ever</u>. To eight within 12 months.

Yes, one can argue that there was an unprecedented amount of cash thrown at the "vaccine" development programs and it seems that the formulae for the "vaccines" were all but ready to go early in 2020 (even before lockdown). But that raised other questions.

It is worth noting that the mRNA trial protocols never sought to monitor the effects that these gene therapies might have on infection or transmission. This was open knowledge. I knew this in the autumn of 2020. Is it really feasible that governments, the FDA, the CDC, etc did not?

Whether knowingly or not, they lied. The President of the USA stated on film that you will not get the virus if you take these "vaccines".

In that context, after decades of failure (both for coronavirus vaccines and mRNA technology), we now had eight coronavirus "vaccines" approved (under EUA) within months.

By whom? By the FDA, MHRA, EMA, TGA, etc. These regulatory bodies worked under the mandate of the governments which they served and which had pre-committed to purchasing billions of dollars of vaccines. They existed inside the figurative skulls of the governments that had guns pointed to their heads by virtue of the historic sacrifices that they insisted their populations make.

Normally, those regulatory bodies sit across the table from the Big Pharma companies. Poacher versus gamekeeper.

This time they were essentially regulating their ultimate masters. Gamekeeper versus employer/estate-owner.

Hundreds of billions of dollars of pre-purchased merchandise were at stake (worthless, if not approved). The galling sacrifices of their populations were at stake (in vain, if not justified).

Those regulatory bodies were in the position of having a veto on the survival of the institutional structures of which they were a wholly-owned, controlled and dependent part.

That is not to say that the above concerns are sufficient grounds for dismissing the "vaccines". Not at all. But I will admit that they went some way, for me, to raising the bar for what I consider to be sufficient evidence that the "vaccines" are appropriate and materially beneficial for me and my family. Especially for those members who I do not deem to be at a material risk from COVID.

I need more than selected/curated experts telling me not to ask questions and to just take it.

I need to have my concerns acknowledged and addressed.

I need to hear debate, a risk/reward assessment. I need transparency on the trial data. I need investigation into any adverse effects. Explanations of how conflicts of interest were mitigated.

Goddamit, I need there to be a clinical system for tracking adverse events. If you can track "vaccination" status via smartphone apps, you can track adverse effects more effectively than VAERS/Yellow Card at the very least.

Instead, we had:

- Trials for which the data are still restricted;
- Trials for which the placebo group was eliminated;
- Trials where a whistle-blower raised the alarm on shocking procedures and practices;
- Focus on relative versus absolute risk;
- Leaders outright lied (presumably knowingly) that the "vaccines" would stop infection and transmission;
- A dismaying, systematic censorship of any challenge;

- A legacy tracking system for adverse events that is voluntary and deeply fallible;
- Lies about only targeting the vulnerable for inoculation;
- Overrule of the FDA's expert panel and resignation of senior executives;
- Selective dismissal of natural immunity;
- "Vaccine" passports despite the demonstrable lack of any benefit;
- Contract disclosures that strongly demonstrate desperate governments with weak negotiating positions;
- Suppression of discussion on early-stage therapeutics or re-purposed drugs as a pre-hospitalisation alternative;
- A one-size-fits-all policy from obese 85-year olds to healthy teenagers (sinisterly, even for children as young as six months);
- Worrying increase in non-COVID excess deaths, initially in Israel after the 2nd booster (4th dose) and increasingly visible in other Western countries.

There are too many inter-related rabbit holes down which I would happily plunge but will spare you the rant on:

- Stratified risk of COVID by age, weight, underlying health conditions;
- Data upon which decisions have been justified (deaths with/of COVID);
- Change in the definitions of a "vaccine", "anti-vaxxer", "pandemic" and "herd immunity";
- Efficacy of PCR tests and cycle thresholds;
- Asymptomatic spread;
- Justification in calling modelling of the future, "science";
- Effectiveness of lockdowns and other NPIs, including masks;
- Avoidance of antibody testing;
- Lockdown harms;
- Preventative supplements;
- Fauci; and
- Just too many more.

It is true. It's true that I have started from a position that was sceptical and circumspect of taking one of the new technology "vaccines". Frankly, I think this is eminently sensible, my deepest moral duty even, for my family and me.

This wariness was housed in the context of my own risk assessment for my family being infected with SARS COV 2 and developing COVID 19 as a result.

As a healthy man of under 50 years old who exercises (a lot), eats well, sleeps well and enjoys being outside, my assessment was that I was at extremely low risk. My immediate family had an even lower risk.

Now that we have all had COVID and have antibodies, I assess this risk to be effectively zero.

You can agree or disagree, but that is my assessment to make. You are most welcome to make your own.

I am amongst the top 0.00001% [estimated!] most vaccinated individuals to have walked the Planet Earth.

These mRNA treatments do not prevent infection nor transmission. They require the injection into my body of unspecified substances.

These are unprecedented medical interventions with no long-term safety data. They are still under Stage 3 clinical trials.

I don't need and I don't want a jab. I question why anyone wants me to have one (seriously – why do you care?). If you put pressure on me, you are being deeply unethical and contravening the Nuremburg code.

I have yet to see a persuasive reconciliation of vax mandates with medical ethics. What happened to our medical ethics?! I hear the Hippocratic Oath is nowadays optional in US medical schools.

So, thanks but no thanks. This assessment may change as more information emerges – but it's not looking good…

And I do…I do wonder if I am indulging in a form of "intellectual" belligerence. Some entity I am not in control of is seeking to assert itself on me. I don't appreciate this form of unearned control and so I push back irrespective of the potential efficacy underpinning that entity's edict.

But no – they want to stick a needle in me and inject unidentified substances into me for a malady which carries minimal risk to me.

So, no…in summary, fuck the fuck off!

Depart

After ploughing through the monumental barrage of stuff to be done, we were there. We had whittled ourselves down to a family of four with a luggage collection that assumed both good weather and only a medium-sized hire car.

It was early July 2021. As our Hong Kong taxi skidded towards the still-deserted airport, I was struck by the surreal sensation of departing our family's home. The surrounding scenes flashing past were so familiar that they will be deeply burned into our long-term memory. For Raf, Hong Kong had been the only country in which we had ever lived. It had been a long time coming but it still felt as if we were fleeing.

We suddenly felt homeless. We knew and could picture our end destination but, between now and then, we had only the very earliest etchings of the picture we were about to collectively paint.

Our taxi journey provided only 40 minutes to dwell upon these sentimentalities. Soon enough, having entered the cavernous checking-in area, we were yanked back to the reality of the present. Having flapped an array of diligently prepared paperwork at the check-in attendant, he unexpectedly asked to see an additional proof. Evidence of our commitment to leave Spain.

We explained our plan, but that did not meet the unwritten regulation. Kate launched into battle on her iPhone, frantically searching for what could be done to tick this unanticipated box. After what felt like an age, we had booked an extra week's car hire from San Sebastien (northern Spain) to Lilles (France). Fellow travellers huffed and puffed behind us, but the check-in man was heroically patient.

Eventually, we flashed him the phone screen. Booking confirmation. One extra week's car hire. Drop-off at Lilles, France. At an additional cost of EUR 1,000. Box ticked, boarding passes printed, queue unblocked.

And, once through security, the EUR 1,000 booking was promptly cancelled.

Just...because.

Spanish Flew

From this point on until departing from Spain, I kept a handwritten journal. This is something I haven't done since I was in my early teens (when evidently I was experimenting, cringingly, with writing the word "fuck").

I loved it. There is something deeply therapeutic about handwriting a daily journal.

Unfortunately, I found that my eagerness to put down for the written record our daily experiences (for posterity...for the KIDS!!) overrode the inclination to pen masterful insights. Maybe there weren't any of those.

It is a question to which I have not yet heard a convincing answer. I have not seen a secondary school yet where the pupils are not learning on devices, iPads or laptops. I am hearing that this is starting to cause notable physical reactions, with children hunched over their screen all day to then go home and do some more on-screen homework. Could it be the case that these hours, days, weeks, years of unnatural posture during the most critical growth years are causing a catalogue of unforeseen posture issues? I know a number of physiotherapists who say it is becoming a problem.

But does it also change how the kids think? How our children will formulate their thoughts in the future? Has anyone looked into this or are we throwing ourselves all-in to this mass experiment?

When penning a written piece, one has to think before one writes. To mentally fine-tune the point being made, compose the sentence in advance, to find the correct words. Occasionally, one has the confidence to launch into a thought or report without cerebrally pre-scripting it but that takes practice.

Our children will have been educated by splattering down thoughts on a screen in the ever-comforting knowledge that they can reverse, auto-correct and adapt what previously would have been permanently inked.

My first journal entry was from Doha.

After a year of not being able to leave Hong Kong, we were suddenly at 2am somewhere completely different. The flight itself had already done much to salve concerns about the World outside Hong Kong. The mask-wearing and enforcement on the flight were half-hearted to say the least. Waiting in transit at Doha airport (in the middle of the night) it was clear that large sections of the rest of the World were getting on with life.

We surreally, hazily fumbled our way through the four hours of wait-time before setting off for the second leg flight to Barcelona. That was another easy journey but, as the blush sunrise asserted itself above the clouds and through the window of row 28, heralding our day of arrival in Spain, a sense of nervous anticipation rose in all of us.

Had we read all the relevant literature, printed out all the required forms, the QR codes, downloaded the right app? Would a UK passport attract the same requirements as an Australian one, had the guidance changed on "vaccinations", PCR tests, RAT tests? Had we missed some small print?

It was daylight, we were off the plane, on the ground in Europe…but would we be allowed in?...

Nothing we had read suggested that this would be easy.

As it was, we glided through the Spanish health security check almost without breaking step. A scan of a QR code and a disarming indifference to the gushing gratitude that flashed across my face prompted a voiceless nod to open the turnstile to España.

The documentation stress that had acted as a permanent weight on our peace of mind dissipated in a moment.

The journey from the airport was a light, happy blur. As the taxi drew into the early morning shadow of the Catalunya Cathedral and in front of the façade of our first World Detour hotel accommodation, we were mildly delirious with optimistic excitement. We indulged in the breakfast feast that was on offer in the baroque dining room, delicious in its elegant simplicity…and its signifying the start of two months of cultural immersion in Northern Spain.

Our days in Barcelona were energised by an underlying acknowledgement that we were at the beginning of a unique four-month chapter of our lives. A thread of stories yet to be written. We were going to be converting our daily experiences into immutable layers of family history.

On the first day, we jumped on the Barcelona City Bus. We visited the zoo, the Aquarium…some of the more obvious, easy-access attractions as we sought to smooth out the creases of jet-lag that present themselves at inconvenient moments!

On the second day, we strolled the 40 minutes it took to the Sagrada Familia.

A magnificent testimony to the creations of which humans are capable. Just so ridiculously wondrous. A formidable monument to the ability of the human mind and collective efforts to produce art that transcends existence in terms of mere survival.

The Boys got it, too. They were properly bowled over. Photographer Rex eagerly snapped an array of intricate features and angles.

The building unashamedly boasts its deep-seated inspiration in nature, its devotion to adopting its strength and resilience from the structures of creation around us.

It's not as if Rex and Raf sat there and ruminated over these impressions but I like to believe that they absorbed the power of art into their souls by osmosis.

We loved Barcelona. It is belligerently, unapologetically itself.

Those first few days outside of Hong Kong were bathed in a balm of relief and optimism. As if we had surfaced from a deep, lung-busting dive. We were out. We had left that segment of our lives permanently behind and, whilst there were certainly frayed, loose ends to which we would need to attend, we were on a new path.

Situated proudly on the ancient, culture-drenched Mediterranean, Barcelona blended its abundantly rich tapestry of ancient wisdom with the modern World of mopeds, glass-fronted offices and vape shops. It was our perfect gateway into our Spanish wonderland.

Rustic Must

Having, each of us, processed our respective jet-lags and indulged in our European city fix, it was time to connect with the Iberian outback.

After a tortuously unnecessary two hours spent processing our hire car, we haphazardly exited Barcelona into the countryside. Haphazardly, because, as we all know, satellite navigation systems like to screw with couples. They surgically identify that line of interpretation that divides the driver and the passenger. Each has an equally valid argument to back their understanding of the electronic instructions provided. This fuels a decision-making volley back and forth over the gear stick that unhelpfully piles additional stress upon that already presented by Spanish traffic.

Of course, the beauty of sat nav is that no-one is ultimately to blame. Had it been the driver or the passenger taking responsibility and subsequently getting lost in the middle of a foreign road system, there would be an undiluted target of blame. The genius of sat nav is that, as an independent third party that denies the right of reply, it can act as the passive scapegoat time and again. It must have been trying to direct us away from a jam or it didn't know that road was closed for roadworks or there may have been a crash, etc.

All of these "outs" allow the two warring interpreters an obvious, latent fall guy. A bit like a recycling bin for plastic bottles, it provides a guilt-purge depository for our own mistakes.

As we found ourselves humming along on increasingly free-flowing roads out of the city, my mind began to wonder how this scapegoating in absentia happens to each of us when we are not there in person to provide some counterbalance to the blame dumping.

Those untidied, loose threads from Hong Kong trickling into my conscience? Maybe.

As motorways morphed into roads, we zipped passed Barcelona's outlying towns and our optimistic anticipation amped. I have always loved the moment when you pick up the keys to a holiday apartment and pause on the threshold of your home for the coming week. I am not sure if it's the novelty of living in a different space, the knowledge that you are about to create memories or that it is as simple as a mental correlation to not being at work.

When we arrived, it was everything that we had wished it to be.

Our temporary home was to be an old farmhouse nestled on the lower fringe of a verdant forest that carpeted the flank of an elongated hill. Numerous tracks webbed into the adjacent woods. Aged trees elicited a sense of calm, composed wisdom – "we've seen it all". I found it irresistible to picture ancient, leather-sandalled goat-herders tracing the same paths as my neon trainers. Clear-minded folk concentrating on their daily, essential activities.

Our kitchen consisted of a massive timber dining table overlooked by a cooking space that lent itself perfectly to the preparation of salads, cold meats, fried chorizo and pimentos padron. The Boys found plenty of nooks, crannies and danger to keep them occupied, freeing me up to explore the surroundings and suck in the fresh, pine air.

In the mornings, I would hike up through the trees to the top of the recumbent hill to take in the sunrise. From this raised plateau, I could survey the valley gently de-mist and unveil itself to the warmth of the new day. Topless (why not) I would break into a run with my arms stretched out on either side.

FREEEEDOOOOM!!!

Bloody hell, that felt good.

In the evenings, we found ourselves drawn into a wonderful routine of constructing an eclectic platter of local produce, accompanied with a chilled glass of the palest rosé…and a game of Uno with Rex and Raf.

With no schedule, no bedtime, no planning for the day ahead it was only the increasing insistence of dusk that brought a gradual end to the silly jokes, good-natured ribbing and competitive score-keeping.

Monastery

I am not religious. To my mild regret, I went along with what was taught as a given at school but, even as I was being confirmed at the age of 16, my critical nature could not ignore the leaps in faith that religion demanded.

However, I have always had a spiritual side. And I have always loved monasteries.

And Monserrat Monastery is simply breath-taking. Foremost, there is the location. The surrounding plateau provides a timeless viewing platform encircling the monolithic rock formation that burst from beneath the Earth's crust 25 million years ago.

Chiselled three quarters of the way up into the side of these almightily imposing, jagged peaks is a human creation of a more modest, if more intricate, nature. The monastery.

We popped into a service. Witnessing the procession of grey-haired men self-servingly chanting Latin psalms whilst clad in gold-laced robes yanked me back to my anti-religious stance. But…is there a meditative quality to the performance which is maybe the point?

There is no doubting the sense of awe that surrounds the place. One can easily argue that this is the wonder of the encompassing nature, not of the monastery. Is it that this deeply impressive Earth-generated shrine to creation has been co-opted by humans seeking to make sense of their place in this World?

Maybe. And certainly, the size of the gift shop suggested that they were eager to milk it!

Wherever you sit on that spectrum of thought, the Montserrat Monastery and its surroundings are utterly magnificent.

Religion versus Spirituality

Weeeell, that's as good a time as any to descend deep into some deckchair philosophy.

And it's a biggie. It's religion!

As touched upon, it's one I have been wrestling with for some time. I reached a point where the demands of religion to depart from rational thinking about what is true forced me to reject those teachings. At least, I thought they did.

I have always considered myself spiritual. Despite rejecting organised religions in my teens, I would say my own version of prayers until well into my thirties.

But I could never succinctly distil what I really felt…felt to be as true as I could be comfortable with. I struggled for a long time to cobble together a coherent explanation of what I believed. I was delighted, on reading *Richard Dawkins' The God Delusion*, to find the definition of a pantheist: the view that the World is either identical to God, or an expression of God's nature.

This provided me both with what seemed like a sufficiently profound defence to drunken interrogations on the subject but also provided a way for me to defer asking myself the more probing questions.

I will be able to think more about that when I finally retire to be surrounded by nature and with the luxury of time, I would say to myself.

A video, a podcast and two books went a long way to shunting me out of that intellectual holding bay.

The YouTube video was the first of a series with Jordan Peterson and Sam Harris on stage in Vancouver debating the question of whether it is possible to construct and adhere to a moral framework without securing the foundations of that structure in religious doctrines.

It is an amazing debate to watch and I would recommend it to anyone with an interest. You can sense the audience becoming increasingly enthralled as the discussion burrows deeper and deeper in search for a spiritual truth. I went through a phase of feeling self-conscious about recommending it to friends but I am very much over that now!

Then I listened to Joe Rogan's podcast with *Brian Muraresku.* I was intrigued enough to read Brian's book, the *Immortality Key.* At the same time, a friend in Hong Kong recommended *Carlo Rovelli's The Order of Time.*

Those two books together have taken me to a new place, where I am currently residing!

The first is like a real World Da Vinci Code search for the mysteries of Eleusis. The author combs the archives, archaeological digs and all other leads around the Mediterranean in an effort to uncover the truth about the spiritual practices followed by the Greeks…and what they were convinced led them to discover the meaning of life.

Essentially, they accessed new realms of perception that allowed them to rise above our four-dimensional World (4th dimension being time). They did this by drinking herb/fungal concoctions that brought on psychedelic episodes. A recurring theme is how difficult it is to put into words the sensations experienced, as they are beyond the everyday experiences to which language has matched. There is a sense of all-encompassing wholeness, timelessness, ubiquitous benevolence and a calming enlightenment. The dissipation of a fear of death is a common theme, as the conviction that our lives are simply a capsule in the subset of dimensions that make up the greater whole.

Man.

But the more I looked into it, the more sources reported the same difficult-to-articulate transcendent experiences.

The book, fascinatingly, goes on to suggest that these insights into supra-life spirituality were suppressed by religions such as Christianity… whilst at the same time, that knowledge was guarded within a narrow, enlightened few.

Similar experiences emanate from trips taken on psylocibin or DMT. And they also resonate closely with near death experiences.

The Order of Time is a poetically-written journey that holds your hand into the mind-bending latest understanding of quantum physics. And then gently leads you back to earth. My overarching, mind-blowing takeaway was that the unavoidable conclusion of quantum theory is that time does not really exist. That there are discreet planck length periods of time in which everything and nothing exists.

Woe, man!

I was relieved to hear Richard Dawkins more recently state that he did not understand quantum theory and, in his view, our minds are not adapted to do so. It's only a few egg-headed physicists with mutated maths brains that can contort their minds into these realms. Which is handy, because I am told the mathematically provable extension of quantum theory is that there are an infinite number of universes (the multiverse) in which every conceivable life we could have lived out is, in fact, being played out.

Blank stare...blink.

So. My current thinking is this. We can only experience that which we are capable of experiencing. We evolved to sense four dimensions. Our 3-D World plus time. We can conceive of a 2-D World but that, in our evolved minds, can only come into being in a 3-D World and then only becomes dynamic in a 4-D realm.

What if there is, in greater reality, a 5, 6, 7...20-dementional World and we just do not have the sensory, thinking equipment to perceive those dimensions in our physical, living state (without psychedelics)?

In our non-trippy everyday mindset, is there an unidentifiable sixth (or is it fifth?) sense that understands that we are part of that broader dimensional state? And is it that instinctive understanding that constitutes our spirituality? That our human sense of being part of a greater whole is exactly that, only we do not have the sensory or verbal tools to describe it.

Do I sound like a hippy? Not sure.

Hey ho – need to find somewhere where I can take some psylocibin!

Vineyard

The owner of our temporary farm home was a fascinating chap. When his father passed away a few years ago, he called time on his successful expat career that saw him then stationed in Brazil.

The sad passing acted as a calling to return home to his 1,000-year-old Catalan farmhouse and accompanying vineyard. As a terrific and timely example of being able to switch livelihood even at an advanced age, he had taught himself what he needed to know to run the winery.

Not to say that it was an easy way of living. The big Rioja operations were dumping a lot of their produce on the market at prices with which smaller producers just could not compete. Our man relied on strong personal relationships with specific restaurateurs, mostly in Barcelona, to see him through what had been a very testing COVID period.

But he was a wonderful host and patiently guided the four of us through his vine-encircled home and colourful family history, laden with antique wine-making equipment...and tales of deathly rifts cleaved by the Spanish Civil War. As we were departing through the car park, he even let Raf have a drive of his small tractor. As if the little terror needs any more encouragement to cause trouble, huh.

The warmth with which he gave up his time and welcomed us into his gripping family history conveyed a geniality that showed itself to be pervasive throughout Catalonia.

By way of a generous (/self-serving) token of gratitude, I loaded up with a crate of his fruity, family white wine and we bade each other, adios!

World View

It is worth mentioning that, throughout these early days of our trip, I was keeping a close (mildly obsessive) eye on what was happening in the World. I was horrified to see how the concept of "vaccine" passports was being normalised. How commentators, whose opinions I had previously respected, had cut anchor and been swept away on a tide of panic-fuelled authoritarianism. Whether it was by virtue of being at arm's length from any specific media, it was palpably obvious that opinion was being orchestrated by the media.

Many a moment, I would develop that stone-in-the-stomach sense of dread when seeing the videos of mass protests across the globe that were simply not reported in the MSM. Just astonishing. Why? Who was making these decisions. To my mind, I could not reconcile the cinematic proof with the silence and obfuscation being presented by the news media to those with less time and/or curiosity to seek for themselves.

I sensed that this meant, in the future, I would be challenged by individuals who had been subject to a different portrayal of the news. Who had only seen the MSM take on the facts. A different truth. A truth fundamentally distinct from mine. Now that we live in a time where truth seems to be in the eye of the beholder.

But I did comfort myself in the cosy echo-chamber of some sensible voices – a Zuby podcast with Nick Hudson of PANDA is one that sticks in my mind from that week.

It was clear to me then that our position on the "vaccine" would make our family a target and cause us problems. How big those problems would be was a big unknown. But there was no question that matters could get very ugly. There was a clear campaign to demonise the unvaxxed. Looking across Europe, across the Western World, it was coordinated. Whatever power lay behind that macro push, we were going to be in its way.

Kate and I did question ourselves: is there a point where the problems being caused are so substantial that we should bite the bullet? Is there an argument to say that the potential physical harm to ourselves would be overshadowed by the negative social consequences for our children?

I don't want to be over dramatic, but isn't that the same reasoning that led French and German citizens to identify Jews to the SS? In any case, that was life and death. This isn't. Yet.

Kate and I agreed that, on point of principle, we just could not acquiesce to this insane, unethical coercion. And if there was no resistance from critical adults, what was to say that they would not seek to push this onto our children?

As we continued our journey into an unsettlingly uncertain second half of 2021, we wondered how many like-minded folk we would come across.

Family Reunion

It was with a wistful regret that I snuck in a final misty sunrise hill-hike before bidding farewell to our first Spanish farmhouse.

It was time to meet my family! A long-yearned for reunion with my adored sister and her family and my beloved mother.

With the unsettling nature of the bendy, skiddy Spanish main roads amplified by the expanding disconnect between the World as seen through the GPS of sat nav and the reality on the ground, our journey was far from chillaxing.

Kate took particular pleasure in my erroneous overruling of our digital orienteer regarding which number exit to take off a roundabout. The rest of the journey consisted of her leading the two Boys on a Spanish count of "unos, dos, tres", etc at each and every opportunity.

That logistical noise did provide sufficient mental distraction to bridge to our arrival...and there, suddenly, was my sister - in person for the first time in 18 months - it was a sudden and deeply familial, loving moment.

It is a strange thing, physically seeing an incredibly close loved one for the first time after a long period...in the age of FaceTime. Such a wonderfully warm, viscerally comforting hug. Sister-brother contact. Yet the moment was accompanied with a disorientating, contradictory feeling that I had only just seen her a couple of weeks ago, when we last spoke to each other online.

A modern phenomenon to which we are yet to attach a label.

I experienced it again when I picked up Mum from the airport. Suddenly, the living, breathing, smiling, talking image on our iPad was sitting in the taxi next to me. There was just as much (and as little) to say as you might do over a screen, just a better 3-D experience. With heat and breeze and background traffic noise. I don't doubt that many a brainstorm is zipping through Silicon Valley as to how best to usher that transition from real life to the...Metaverse!

Anyway, our family reunion week in Tarragona was everything that you might expect it to be. It was just wonderful to be back in the warm, heart-beating bosom of the people to whom I belong the most, next to my own genetic kin!

Rex and Raf played beautifully with their cousins and it was as if they had never been apart. Having a swimming pool to hand throughout also provided a permanent source of entertainment, limited only by exposure time in the sun.

Naturally, whenever families from different routines come together to share their 24-hour rhythms there are tensions. R&R were constantly working on manipulating events so that they could share in / have a turn on their cousin's "tech".

Where Barcelona sought to marry ancient history with modern city living, Tarragona was a town where antiquity collided with 20th century industrialisation. There, carved into the enduring Mediterranean shoreline the gently lapping, hypnotic waters provided an ageless backdrop to the stunning Roman amphitheatre. Visions came to me of long summer evenings under a black, star-studded blanket ceiling of wonder. The venue packed with an appreciative, tunic-wearing audience eager to indulge in a comic-tragedy delivering profound quandaries to be pondered for weeks thereafter.

But look up now and you see that a railway track had been planted in between the arena and the sea and, a little further into the distance, a commercial port was unapologetically getting on with its daily, 21st century grind.

Of course, of course the Big "C" was discussed at length. My sister, bless her, took a lot of my points on the "vaccine" but her overriding issue was that our family's stance might mean we would not see each other very easily over the coming years.

For the same reason that FaceTime provided a sense of having seen each other recently, we were all pretty up-to-date with each other's stances on the 'Rona and the bounty of other divisive issues with which we are being poisoned! I am glad – no, eternally grateful - to say that my sister and I have found a way to have disagreements on some of the most emotive subjects over the years without falling out. I think that may be a result of us knowing each other well enough to understand that we ultimately have the same targets in mind – it's just that we see different modes of getting there.

Whilst the week zipped past in a flurry of BBQs, swimming and lounging by the end of it, a comfortable understanding had emerged that we were all ready to part ways and again do our own thing.

Light drizzle marked the morning we left with a sprinkle of nostalgia, recognising that our vastly anticipated reunion had come and gone - nostalgia anaesthetised by the knowledge that we would all see each other again in the UK in a matter of weeks.

Auto Books

A few years back, Kate and I mercilessly "broke" the Boys in terms of them enduring long distance car journeys. Kate's parents live a five-hour drive from Brisbane and being strapped in, facing backwards for a couple of hours at a time meant that toddler cries of boredom had to be ignored to the point of the emitters exhausting themselves into silence.

But we hadn't launched into a long road trip for a very long time and the two Boys had become used to managing their backseat boredom by manufacturing increasingly vicious arguments out of the slightest territorial infringement.

It's not new, the age-old cliché of parents yelling at their post-toddler kids in the back of the car. However, for those of you who have not yet discovered this, Kate and I stumbled upon a magical life-saver.

Audio books.

We didn't know this would work but I had already found myself over-excited about the endlessly rich, ancient cultural history surrounding us. As a result, I suggested an audiobook based on the Greek myths (who doesn't love them?!). After some expert fumbling through options on her iPhone, Kate found a children's version of the origin of the Greek Gods.

Little were we to know then that this would not only become a road-rescuing readathon but that it would also lead to a far-reaching obsession with all stories, films, costumes Greek and Roman in the coming years.

Kate and I also absolutely loved re-learning the 12 (+1) gods and goddesses. Their amazing talents as well as their all-too-human flaws. Their privileged and slanted, if humanly understandable, moral codes.

Worryingly, if predictably, Raf took a particular shine to Hades. I determinedly claimed Dionysus.

This classical exploration also led to some fabulous family conversations. Who could miss the similarities of Prometheus having his liver pecked out and that of the spear in Christ's side? Or Zeus's attempt to flood humanity and Deucalion's ark mirroring that of Noah, etc.

Is there an early, underlying religious sexism that saw the 50:50 male:female ratio of the 12 Olympian gods morph into Christianity's 12 all-male apostle line-up?

Is it really feasible that the direct resemblances between these foundational stories are by chance rather than via Christianity building on the eternally captivating Greek myths – a belief-bridge emanating from the mists of our deeper, pe-historic past?

Thankfully, the Boys had a selective hearing capability that allowed them to zone out our amateur parental hypothesising. They were able to lock into the narration, finding the stories captivatingly enchanting... beguiling. They would disappear into their own minds, their personal representations of the tales being hosted in a technicolour wonderland unique to their own, singular headspaces.

Whilst they were not reading, they were being wonderfully taught the gift of story-telling – the power of a yarn. The bringing to vivid life of characters, scenes, emotions and meanings. At the same time, were some of the deeply moral, ethical and human dilemmas being seeded into their subconscious? As they have been into countless children over millennia.

Suddenly, we would arrive at our destination. But the chapter would not have finished. So on a number of occasions, we would have to let the Boys – even after a monster four hour drive – sit in our stationary vehicle in the driveway in order to reach an acceptable break in their enchantment.

Next

It was a car full of minds whirring with images of the Titans that arrived in the mountains behind El Port de la Selva. After some time-pressured internet surfing we had come across a six-day opening at a stunning farmhouse in a village first formed in 1200, La Vall de Santa Creu. Other than the giveaway electrical wires skipping from house to house, this was a step back in time. Our home for the next week was hewn out of medieval stone and exuded the wise permanence of its weathered history.

Appliances and decorations were also from a time long past.

A small breakfast terrace appeared mostly functional until one looked up and saw that it was permanently presided over by the imposing, everlasting Monasterio de Sant Pere de Rodes. Its origin as a monastic cell in 878 was built upon in the 11th and 12th centuries to construct this robust statement of imperial permanence at the summit of the overshadowing mountain.

As the week ticked over, I would enjoy a morning coffee as the sun gently warmed the small quad, looking up to its elegant façade, like a schoolboy to his sporting idol, and I would have a think. Think about what had happened in the World since this mightily impressive building first assumed its statuesque position.

The World was currently flapping around hysterically about a bug that was, for the vast majority, a bad cold. Yet this monolith of commanding certainty had seen off the bubonic plague, the Black Death, the Dark Ages, eruption of Vesuvius, the coming and going of the Aztec Empire, Genghis Khan, the Ottoman Empire, the discovery of the New World, the Spanish Civil War, both World Wars, electricity, the steam engine, etc, etc.

Wherever disturbances might be occurring on the planet, this monument to continuity did not flinch.

I loved to sit there and wonder, what else will it see off.

Crazy Klaus Schwab, a digital currency, a bio-surveillance state, mass depopulation, terraforming Mars, transhumanism…ahhhh?!?!?

There is most definitely something humbling and meditative about contemplating a manmade structure that has withstood so much passing of time. So many sunrises. So many breakfast chair philosophers attempting to pin down their wandering thoughts.

El Port De La Selva

But, goodness me, what a wonderful part of the World. It was only a short drive to the nearest town, El Port de la Selva. A fully functioning, Olde Worlde fishing village. A church clock that chimed every 15 minutes.

Fishing boats chugged in, chugged out of the small port. Nets were repaired. Fruit and vegetables were delivered to the market. A constant bustling of locals setting about their daily tasks.

And every 15 minutes the church clock would clang.

The constant reminder of time passing was itself timeless.

The Boys learned to fish. And were a lot less squeamish than I expected.

Having secured our coffees and allocated our flaking croissants amongst the family, we decided on a spot along the jetty. After some intensely inexpert preparations, we began amateurly prodding the glistening surface with hooks sporting sorry- and very dead-looking sardines bought from the local fishmonger.

In our minds' eyes we were well set up...up and running and fishing. Just a matter of time. However, we were soon masterminded out of our ignorance by the Grumpy-Kind Man!

A Mediterranean architype, our new grey-haired friend proudly boasted a lovingly curated pot belly. With smiling implicitly dismissed as a pointlessly shallow affectation of glib people (I am projecting), he communicated with minimal gesticulation and the occasional grunt.

He had seen us and had voluntarily come to help us out. That was communication enough.

After a wordless tutorial that would have bridged any language barrier, time interval or cultural gap, Rex and Raf had fresh sardines, a strong steer as to where best to stand and a far better idea of at what depth to float the bait.

And it worked! Almost immediately.

Rex's reaction was disbelieving, blind panic.

Mine was to abandon grappling with Raf and his newly baited line and to fumble for my phone camera.

Moment captured. A seminal moment for me. A father-son rite of passage! A sense of gratification blossomed for we had just caught our first fish together (an act as ancient and symbolic as any for homo sapiens) in this stunning time capsule…embedded in scenery that had witnessed the birth of Western culture…

Just too much!

I was brusquely tugged back down to earth with a hollow thud as, out of the corner of my eye, the motion of Raf's rod leaping off the jetty and into the sea caused my head to snap in that direction.

He had caught one too!! Or rather, would have, had his over-excited father actually maintained some morsel of composure.

As it was, his rod handle stuck out at a 45-degree angle, about ten metres out to sea. Like a feeble, watery Excalibur.

Kate was angry. Apoplectic. Incandescent. So consumed by rage that her body convulsed into a satanic, hopping foetus with clenched fists.

I had only seen this once before but this time (in stark contrast to the first) we both laughed and promptly dispensed with all and any dignity in order to right this amateur's error.

In a cringe-worthy, Hugh Grant esque gush of apologia, I managed to persuade a passing French family that had neared the jetty in a dinghy to put-put out to the "cane de peche" and retrieve it for us.

That's a proper, modern-day hunter gatherer performance, I said to myself. Selflessly discarding my self-respect to problem-solve with a results-based focus – dignity be dammed!

Thankfully, Raf caught a load more fish once we had retaken possession of his rod.

The fish (annular bream, we think) were too small to keep and we had to dehook them to then set them free. This was something with which the Boys – surprisingly for me - were fine. They kept asking whether they had caught enough fish to feed our family and for how many days. It is difficult to overstate how thrilled they both were.

I could not help thinking, how many times had such a process taken place – a Grumpy-Kind Man sharing his knowledge with eager youngsters, helping them catch their first fish in the lapping, sun-soaked fringes of the Mediterranean.

Ancient Wisdom

Spending many hours, rod in hand, contemplating the basic pleasure provided by fishing with my young sons, I had already worked myself into flappy excitement about rediscovering the ancient wisdom of civilisations past.

I mentioned previously that I had already awoken an insistent interest in psychedelics. Had psychedelic-driven trips been the trigger for the consciousness of homo sapiens (the "drunken monkey" hypothesis)? Was the source of human spirituality the drug-induced capability for experiencing our existence through a medium beyond the four dimensions we consciously perceive?

Did the ancients, through ergot-laced beers and wines, find a method of accessing alternate spheres of perception that we might call spirituality?

But now, back down to the Spanish earth, other questions arose. Those that had also been forensically examined, tested, debated, analysed and re-analysed over hundreds, even thousands of years.

Structures of democracy, the meaning of life, good versus bad, pacifism versus aggression, education versus schooling, true wealth versus being monetarily rich.

All of these questions, pivotal to a healthy framing of our lives, had been vigorously assessed by brilliantly sophisticated minds with forensic clarity in an era that predates religions. Religions that seek to short-cut rational thought in favour of demanding unscientific faith.

Could it be that religions have acted as a barrier to rational spirituality?

Sorry, that's a bad question. Rather, was it the case that the religious elites' lack of belief in the proletariat being able to understand the profound lessons upon which religious teachings are based led them to insist on a suspension of rational analysis and to insist on the leap of faith?

Can it be that the majority of us can, in fact, reach the conclusions and meanings underpinning the main faiths through rational thought and analysis?

And why, in our modern era, are we not accessing the vast body of profound wisdom so diligently collated by our ancient ancestors?

At a time when we are being emotionally harassed into feeding off insects and pricing out the poor from access to life-preserving energy, why are we not instead providing to our young an alternative way of understanding and seeing the World?

The Stoics (300 BC) posited that true happiness comes from four virtues: wisdom, justice, courage and moderation. They understood that material goods and external pleasures mean nothing compared to one's own ability to be content based on these simple principles. Principles that map closely to the foundations of most of the leading religions.

And yet, we live in the 2020s where our children are sent to school to rote learn information that will be peripheral (at best) to their lives.

Rather than standing on the shoulders of giants, we drill them into being intellectual Lilliputians.

One could argue that organised religion and its faith dictat caused an over 1,000-year delay in the Enlightenment. One could also argue that an authoritarian reaction to the Enlightenment has caused our current regressive Endarkenment.

The youth of today are not taught to think for themselves. There are no classes on philosophy, entrepreneurship, growing produce, critical thinking or even rational logic. The young are treated as empty hard drives that need to be filled up with information to pass a government-designed MOTs (motor operation test) so as to allow them to explore only on designated, speed-limited roads.

They are programmed with disposable hardware. Not self-learning, anthropic intelligence.

We have somehow ended up delegating future creative transformation to Silicon Valley's artificial version.

It seems to me that if we could convince just a proportion of our youngsters to think more and to consume less, that this would be spectacularly more beneficial for the physical and intellectual World that we live in than the bankrupting policies currently being pursued.

Rather than being taught to pass exams to generate meaningless grades that act as access codes to a life chasing paper, fiat money in a corporation designed to obsess only about perpetuating itself, why not find a purer happiness in a simple life?

To consider rather than consume?

Expo-sed

My memories of El Port de la Selva will be forever smothered in a hallowed shroud of Mediterranean white and pale blue. We spent six glorious days nestled in a village that time forgot (or at least let slip by), monitored fatherly by a monastery that spanned civilisations, never mind generations. The initial thrill of catching our first fish effortlessly morphed into a patient seaside meditation that did not wear thin over our ensuing daily visits.

Even on the day we departed to head west, we squeezed in a swift session of fishing before launching into the five-hour drive to Zaragoza.

For me, Zaragoza was somewhat of a disappointment.

Much like modern schooling, it was an example of how the old and the new is sometimes not well blended.

The main architectural centre was indeed stunningly beautiful. Ornate and stylish. And, inevitably, touristy.

However, across the river was an expansive concrete wasteland. Tufts of weed broke through the cement paving supporting the 12-foot metal barriers which had been erected to keep folk from straying too close to crumbling buildings. I remember the Aquarium being an excellent experience but that was a rare oasis in a drought-stricken landscape.

This was the aftermath of Expo 2008.

Vast amounts of cement and optimism had clearly been poured into its creation. But maybe a lack of foresight. Whilst Barcelona had presented an organic mingling of old with new, Zaragoza demonstrated the bleak reality of what can happen when authorities force the issue.

Thankfully, we had only arranged to stay for a couple of nights.

For the sake of completeness, and also some travel advice, do not bother visiting Pamplona unless you want to box a bovine at the annual festival. Outside of the bull run, our visit felt like a field trip to a failed social housing project. In fact, we only slept in our hotel and used it as a base for a day trip to San Sebastien (still a solid drive away).

San Sebastien had the air of an old school San Tropez. Lots of wealthy Spanish and French (am I allowed to say, Basque?) sashaying along the crescent-shaped promenade with time to kill. We spent hours and hours playing on the Beach of La Concha. The Lads were engrossed and found the fast-incoming tide ("flood" in their imaginations) the most exciting plaything.

Also notable was the spontaneous anatomy class to which Rex and Raf were exposed. Whilst the World elsewhere was clawing out its own eyes over the question of wearing a cloth rag over one's nose, there were more than a handful of San-bathers whose entire clothing covered less surface area than a face mask.

Whilst the Boys were building wonderfully intricate sandcastles, I was treated both to a greying man unabashedly swapping skimpy swimmers for more palatial post paddle shorts and also to what, after some contemplative sifting through the memory banks, I confirmed to myself was my first live, non-professional lesbian kiss. Which quickly morphed into quite a raunchy mauling.

The Boys, thankfully, missed that. I will tell them about it when they are older.

Fine Whine

Post Pamplona our tour marched on to the much anticipated (by me) mini excursion to the Rioja region. Villabuena de Alava.

Hurrah!

All the time in the background, mostly on social media but also in the online newspapers, a constant drumbeat ramped up the pressure for everyone to get "vaccinated". A skilfully crafted narrative developed designed to guide the thus guidable to blame the unvaxxed for the ongoing "pandemic" and the necessary restrictions. Shamelessly, the phrase "a pandemic of the unvaccinated" was coined and propagated into general consciousness.

The ticker tape of news stories reinforcing this line would leave me feeling helplessly aghast. Western governments had imposed the most insane, totalitarian restrictions on previously free populations - in direct contradiction to pandemic response procedures built on decades of experience – and their ongoing implementation was alleged to be the fault of folk not willing to inject into their veins an unidentified substance that was under a rushed emergency use approval…for a bug that really was only significantly dangerous for the already ill.

The "othering" was in full swing. The Merriam Webster dictionary changed its definition of "anti-vaxxer" to include those who were against "regulations mandating vaccines". This was after, of course, they had already changed the definition of a "vaccine"!

What the hell was going on?

And then there was the realpolitik...again, I noted in my journal that Kate and I were facing a choice between:

- Intellectual integrity, standing up for what we believe in and being able to look the Boys in the eye in the future; or
- A comfortable, socially more acceptable but ultimately dishonest existence (with maybe long-term side effects).

On the same day some deranged New Zealand politician farted out of her mouth some cretinous nonsense that neighbours should not talk to each other in the supermarket.

And such was the constant underlying whirlpool of debate inside my head. On the one hand, the horrific reality of what was being done, however insane, and how that might affect our family was evident. On the other was the confronting challenge of accepting these nonsensical edicts from - I don't know - brainwashed, governmental lickspittles?... or genuinely evil power junkies?

But HEY...we were in Rioja and what better place to indulge in a taster or two of Tempranillo. The Boys clearly clocked the momentousness of the situation after I booked us in for a six-course meal at a nearby vineyard, Baigorri, and behaved well enough for it to be a very enjoyable lunchtime treat.

I do, like so many of us, love a good glass of red wine. I love the look, the smell, the taste, the effect, the link to the past. How it enhances food, the conversations it powers and the ideas it catalyses.

Yes, some utterly stupid, some instantly regrettable but also others deeply profound.

These were the musings that kept me occupied later that afternoon as I sat to the side of the wonderfully active Villabuena town square. The

Boys were thoughtful enough to disappear, playing in the distance, as I beamed glassily at my *final* glass of Rioja and people-watched the various scenes of old men playing cards, corresponding old ladies on a separate table airing their thoughts and views and a broad age spectrum of kids - just generally mucking about.

It is one of those topics that Kate and I have discussed many a time. How much more natural it is for kids across all ages to play with each other. How this aspect is engineered away by most school systems that insist on age segregation. How this stifles the opportunities for older kids to mentor younger kids, younger kids to set their physical and imaginative selves against those of older kids…how kids of the same age can be at vastly different stages of social- and play-learning whereas, likewise, kids from different age groups can get along like a house on fire.

I had been sufficiently intrigued by these questions to read the book *Free to Learn* by *Peter Gray* which presents a captivating argument as to how unnatural today's industrial-style education is. I found it a deeply convincing read and loved the idea of providing more autonomy to the child as to how they want to learn - allowing a child's own and obviously innate drive to educate themselves to flourish in an environment where they have the resources to discover answers for themselves or through consulting with other children or through guidance from facilitating adults.

I loved the concept of empowering children by giving them the responsibility to open-endedly investigate what they are currently finding worthy of more research.

Contrast this with our Western school environments where the bell drills its way into the learning environment, immediately slamming down the shutters on whatever imaginarium is enrapturing the young child's attention. The faceless, unchallengeable audio-edict demands that the child robotically, obediently moves on to an entirely different subject. Their mind might be exploding with an eruption of multi-coloured excitement, ideas and possibilities. But no. The blare of the factory hooter dictates that the time is up on that personal world of discovery and it is time to lock it away in cold storage until the next time.

Genuinely…how can that be a good thing? And how did we end up doing this to our children?

Creativity is cut short. Deep engagement is repeatedly, mechanistically curtailed and actively dis-rewarded. Instead, obedience to a pre-programmed, pervasive alarm is prioritised over any individualistic activity in which the still forming child's mind is engrossed.

Overruled. Klaxon says no. Put it away, move on. Next!

The more you think about it, the more you realise that our current idea of schooling is clinically insane.

And that is just for the early years schooling.

Headline in the FT that afternoon, as I mull these thoughts by the Villabuena de Alava village square: "Tony Blair: How To Vaccinate The World".

Urgh. Back to reality.

We move on to the medieval castle town of Olite!

Medieval Jewel

Next up on our World Detour was the beautiful, historic castle of Olite. We were staying at the *parador* inside the castle walls and it required a couple of tentative attempts before we realised that we did, indeed, have to drive through the castle gates in order to be able to unpack at the entrance of our accommodation for the next three nights.

As we gingerly guided our car around tight, stone buttresses and nudged through throngs of distracted revellers it became clear that our visit had coincided with some type of event. A quick Google revealed that we had the happy good fortune of coinciding our family castle weekend with the annual Medieval Festival celebration!

The Boys immediately slotted into the effervescent spirit of the day and were begging to be able to buy some of the medieval costumes and weaponry on display.

As an unashamedly child-like father I had to admit, it was pretty cool clobber. The wooden swords were beautifully made and items that combined genuine craftsmanship with battle-ready utility. The shields, also solidly crafted out of local wood and boasting coats of arms to match Rex and Raf's imagined allegiances, were built to last.

Kate and I could not resist and we eventually bargained with the Boys that they were each allowed one weapon, a shield and a knight's tunic as long as they conceded that these gifts formed the major portion of their imminent birthday presents.

The Lads have almost exactly two years age-difference, their birthdays being only three calendar days apart. This can be a good and a bad thing. It provides the opportunity to blend the obligatory birthday celebrations into one joint, stress-fest hit. At the same time, it blurs their individual birthday memories which I suspect will become more of an issue as they get older.

Anyway, I immediately extracted enough personal joy from the costumes to justify their expense. The Boys dressing up created a wonderful connection between a nomadic, touristy, expat family and the ancestral celebration unfolding around us - a history of knights, shining armour, wars, treasures and the terrible clashes that set the backdrop to Catalonian identity.

Rex and Raf set about sword-fighting wherever there was enough elbow space. Raf would perform a wonderful pirouette before dramatically making an elaborate, telegraphed lunge with his blade as Rex responded by voicing a unique soundtrack to accompany thrusts and counterthrusts. The silvery moon slid past the *parador* clocktower as dusk cast a shadow of timelessness over the ancient stone arena. As they improvised their blade-wielding choreography, the Boys had fully transported themselves into being the knights behind their shields…they were in the moment. And it was for moments such as these that we had come on our World Detour.

After a sound night's sleep in our creaky, wood-panelled bedrooms (Kate and I were each in a two bedder with one of the Boys, as the ghostly, Olde Worlde nature of the *parador* was understandably spooky for them) the Sunday proved to be the crescendo.

Throughout the festivities, troops of dressed-up musicians would trail around the narrow castle streets reminding us how far music had come since the middle-ages. The protagonists seemed blissfully care-free, with that bliss becoming ever care-freer as they combined imbibition with celebration.

As the afternoon blended into evening the atmosphere raised itself to that of a raucous, devil-may-care beerhall…if you closed your eyes, you could almost imagine yourself back 500 years in time.

Our Sunday evening consisted of enjoying a beer/rosé or two as the Boys combined with a number of the Spanish boys to perform a balletic sword fight. As the sun reluctantly slipped below the castle fortifications the reality of the imminent working week appeared ever less relevant to the locals who were just too busy enjoying the now.

Age Old Problems

One of the priceless benefits of our World Detour was spending just so much time with the Boys. The luxury of unrestricted hours allowed for unrushed, meandering conversations about any topic that might have flicked a switch in their wired minds.

Discussions with Rex and Raf would naturally flow into questions over the esteemed Greek and Roman times. The logical next question of what came of them? How, after over a thousand years of enlightened civilisation, a subsequent period saw disintegrating infrastructure, decayed societies, quantum leaps backwards in education, a relative void in philosophy, scientific discovery and the like.

It still blows my mind to think of some wolf pelt-wearing Visigoth during the Dark or Middle Ages meandering in and out of Roman ruins in deepest Shropshire, aqueducts in the Dordogne or bath houses on the Dalmation Coast and not having the faintest clue how those structures were built. Not knowing where to start in trying to construct one. Or maybe even that they were of any benefit. Too bloody busy trying to stay alive!

Somehow, all that technology, knowledge and cross-generational communication, built on thousands of years of accumulated trial and error, went to shit.

Arguably, much like the technology used to build the pyramids, Machu Picchu and many other ancient constructions that still baffle experts to this day.

Together, we imagined a modern-day version of that Visigoth. Maybe a disease (!) wiped out all the 21st century developed civilisation leaving only hunter gather tribes, such as the Masai Mara or Piripkura of the Amazon, to wonder, in blank amazement, through a derelict New York…in and out of the crumbling lobby of the Empire State building…

degrading computer terminals rendered utterly obsolete by the absence of anyone knowing what to do with them.

Raf and I found these ideas fascinating and we Google-drilled down into the hypothesised five causes leading to the demise of Europe into the Dark and then the Middle Ages:

1) Fall of the Roman Empire;
2) Medieval Ice Age;
3) Famine;
4) Plague; and
5) Lack of good roads.

Strikingly, and without too much of a leap, a number of these dynamics can easily be read across to events unfurling across our World today.

"History doesn't repeat itself but it often rhymes." – Mark Twain

I don't doubt that this will be a heinously amateurish over-simplification of a topic on which a swathe of exalted academics will have penned rivers of heavily researched sagacity, but here goes my version!

[Deep breath]

Fall of the Western Empire!

1) Fall of the Roman Empire

I am going to glibly distil this down to being due to empire overreach – through planned economy and unfulfillable political promises that ultimately led to the loss of control over currency.

Aaaaaaaand, here we are today!

I was always going to launch into another rant about the current state of our governments but this is going to focus on what I increasingly think has been one – if not the – prime drivers for the mess we are currently in.

My contention is this: the design of our financial monetary system by a group of powerful elites has caused a cascade effect that has dictated the very structure of our societies.

Most of these thoughts were fluttering in mind but reading *The Creature from Jekyll Island* by *G. Edward Griffin* and *The Bitcoin Standard* and *The Fiat Standard,* both by *Saifedean Ammous,* in quick succession helped me pin them down. I find the arguments in those books compelling and they ring true with my own experiences…in the system. And now, I can't help but see how the monetary system that was artificially set in train in 1913 has dictated the very structure of our lives.

Starting from the time the Greeks and then the Romans were in power, the known World had pretty much settled on gold and silver as being ubiquitous forms of money. An intermediary store of value that could travel across time and geography to then be traded into other goods or services. These metals were scarce, non-corroding and recognisable across the trading World. They convey no counterparty risk, meaning their value lies in the very asset you are holding (in contrast to modern day cash deposits).

Ultimately, in the bimetal dual, gold won the fight over silver as the currency that was always going to take precedence. The reason for this is that gold is rarer and, as a result, easier to move across distances in volume (more value transported per kilogram).

If only politicians and people had just left gold as money alone, our current World would be a very different place. Under a gold standard a person's efforts and creativity generated value. That value could be exchanged into gold which then could be relied upon as a true store of that value. The gold could be depended upon to provide the individual with food or clothing or shelter, today or many years into the future. It provided relative certainty that the value one created today could be stored to provide for needs in the future. In this way, a productive person could secure their future via hard work when they were most productive. Indeed, once that assurance was achieved, they would be free to risk their additional efforts on entrepreneurial exploits.

The more productive an individual, the more likely they were to achieve future security faster and so were more able to direct their abilities towards other or new value-creation activities.

In this way, the gold standard self-selected for the most productive and efficient amongst us to have more time and energy to direct at more experimental actions that had a chance of furthering human flourishing.

The certainty provided by a unit of gold remaining of similar exchangeable value far into the future incentivised hard work, saving and – once that was at a sufficiently comfortable level – investment.

There was no need for monetary policies in different jurisdictions or centrally controlled interest rates. Gold was gold was gold. Investments were judged on their risk/reward profile based on the solid foundations of certain money.

However!!...what we got instead was a central bank system led by the US Dollar. But not one backed or limited by an asset of value such as gold (a "hard" currency) but rather one backed simply by the "full faith and trust" in the government issuing that currency (a "soft" currency – essentially an IOU saying, please trust me). And one where the price of capital (the interest rate) is not determined by the market but rather by centralised technocrats at the Federal Reserve.

This has meant that the most important price of anything, the price of everything, the cost of money – of time and energy - is centrally planned. The Federal Reserve dictates the interest rate of the reserve currency of the World, the US Dollar, and in so doing impacts the price of every other fiat currency. This in turn decides the trade-weighted value of all the goods and services in those respective countries. We live in a centrally-banked and planned economy.

Soft, fiat currencies are essentially not linked to any underlying creation of value. Left to fend for itself in a free market, fiat money would be wiped out in favour of a hard currency as people would prefer to own and use a form of money that could not be created at a whim by governments.

A soft currency is de-linked from the real World. The government can keep printing it to fulfil the expensive promises with which it bribed the voters in the first place. And because politicians will always cumulatively offer voting populations more and more bribes, they will print more and more soft currency until that value ends up being relatively worthless.

The value will be inflated away over time.

The purchasing power of one US Dollar in 1913 now has the purchasing power of 5 cents.

Inflation is the equivalent of a tax, only by a means of stealth that the majority of those being impoverished do not understand.

'Twas ever thus.

In Roman times, inflation happened through coin-clipping so that less gold was argued to be worth the same as its pre-clipped value. Or the same effect was achieved by blending the gold with other cheaper metals of a similar appearance.

Nowadays, in order to prevent their soft currencies from being blown away by hard currencies, governments have to decree by law that they be used as a medium of exchange. Governments have made it a legal requirement that their citizens pay taxes in that jurisdiction with their soft currency. They also made it a legal requirement that the soft currency be accepted as a means by which a debt can be extinguished. It became illegal to refuse the government's soft currency. These legal requirements were made by decree – by fiat. Otherwise, they would not have survived. We now have a system of soft, fiat currencies imposed by law.

And the fascinating thing for me was that people understood this hundreds, if not thousands, of years ago. Men and women of the World understood that, if there wasn't an asset-linked restraint to a currency, the human urge of governors to print in order to spend in order to convince people to keep them in power was irresistible.

In addition, the reliance only on hard, gold-backed currencies limited wars to those that governments could fund. Because governments could not print money but had to raise funding for their war through taxes or borrowing (the latter being the equivalent to taxing future generations – our children), this demanded implicit agreement for the war effort by the underlying population being taxed.

Hard currencies anchored to an asset of underlying value acted as a restraint on wars.

1913 proved to be a turning point in recent history that set us on a path towards unbounded, inflation-funded wars. In that year, the Bank of England issued a war bond to help fund World War I. But the good citizens of the UK didn't want that war. So, they didn't buy the bond.

As a result, the UK government secretly bought the two thirds of the bond that the market had rejected. The UK state created and bought their own debt (the documentation revealing this only came to light in 2017). They broke from the gold standard. In a time where the British Pound and the US Dollar ruled the monetary World, this was the first domino to fall.

In fact, the Founding Fathers of the US Constitution understood the evils of fiat currency only too well and outlawed its use in their drawing up of that mighty document. It took 125 years of political wrangling, power-broking and confected crises to bring the Federal Reserve Act into being in 1913. This Act was the legislative vehicle that inevitably was incrementally watered down over decades until finally the US Dollar was fully de-linked from gold in 1971. Another domino.

It was largely the vast expense of the Vietnam War, ever less supported by the US taxpayers, that generated a conflict-driven need for the US government to raise more money than the population was willing to afford.

There is an important discussion to be had as to what extent protracted wars are only possible because of the availability of fiat money. In hard currency times, wars would not be fought in towns or cities, as this was where the people and the value that was being fought over were concentrated. And there would be little point in winning a war that led to less value being gained than was being put at battle-risk. The leaders would lose all legitimacy from their populations if they put families' possessions and livelihoods at risk. Instead, warring factions would find a battlefield at a discreet location and have their ruck out there. As soon as it became clear that one side was losing, both sides would negotiate land/gold and move on. They were necessarily constrained by the capital for which they were fighting and, thus, ultimately the approval of their people.

Soldiers would not give their lives if there was nothing left for which to fight and leaders would be signing their own death warrants if they tried to force them to do so.

In essence, the market (roughly) set a limit for destruction and the loss of life.

In contrast, fiat currency has allowed leaders to extract every last penny from their people for the pursuit of war without their agreement – via money printing. Printing of new, unearned notes means that the incremental cost to the government of more weapons and ammunition is zero. It is borne by their taxpayers without their consent. The same dynamic values the towns and cities being fought over at zero. Any cost-benefit analysis is taken out of the decision-making process. Warmongers can (and did…and do) lapse into the sunk cost fallacy and extract wealth from their unknowing populations to then destroy the opposing country's assets until there is nothing left.

Would WW II, the Vietnam, Afghanistan and Iraq wars have lasted as long as they did if they had required their populations to sign off on the money required to fund them? The Russia-Ukraine war would have been over long ago.

As I mithered earlier, the USA has obligations outstanding equivalent to over $750,000 per taxpayer. It seems to me that the "full faith and trust" in the US government might be about to be tested.

Or more likely, the obligations of developing countries to whom the US Dollar fiat debt has cascaded will be tested. And we will see if that breaks the soft money system in its totality. Or will we allow the power-brokers to dupe us into CBDCs?

Fiat debt was always going to escalate until eventually the system explodes. The Fall of the Dollar Empire?

2) The Medieval Ice Age

Without the technology nor the energy to power that technology, our medieval ancestors were left fully exposed to the ravages of the pernicious elements in what was a significantly colder period. Peasants were already living at the margins of survival and the increased time and energy required to protect themselves from the deadly cold absorbed their waking hours.

In contrast, in our modern era, vast swathes of the World's population have had sufficient energy to ensure their protection and resilience against climate/weather-driven dangers.

However, now it appears that those with the critical natural resources (Russia, Brazil...Saudi Arabia?) are at either kinetic or financial war with those without (Europe?). There is a renewed focus on those regions without the ability to protect themselves from the elements whose life-threatening harshness we appear to have all but forgotten. There is a calamitous fissure in the allocation of live-giving food and energy. As I write, we are seeing tectonic shifts in the global balance of power. Where the link between paper monetary wealth and underlying resources have been the weakest, so there are the greatest concerns. Where energy used to flow freely from excess to deficit countries, obstacles have arisen. Where previously we saw rational, diplomatic debate, we are seeing worryingly entrenched positions.

Maybe we are seeing that the relative power of a country ultimately depends on the extent to which it is underpinned by the value it can create from the resources within its borders? Are we seeing a colossal reappraisal and appreciation of the basic building block of human life, energy? Be that first and foremost in the form of fuels that allow us to generate food, heating, cooking, shelter, the production of clothing and other essentials.

Are we going to see countries with the real, tangible means of heating and feeding their people go toe-to-toe with those who built their economies on a house of credit cards?

No-one knows how this is going to play out, but it does feel starkly as if we are living through an historic inflection point in how the World is constructed – in the World Order and how that will look as we plunge deeper into the digital age.

Addictive computer games, on-line courses, school laptops for 12-year-olds, a perpetual blizzard of on-line registrations, QR codes, digital IDs, cashless societies, CBDCs.

A Media-Evil Device Age?

3) Famine

The energy required to protect us from the elements is the same that allows us to feed our huge populations. And, for the first time in my life, people are talking about food shortages and large parts of the World going hungry.

Whilst it seems that the mainstream media is rigidly flooding the airwaves with a single, reductive take, I don't think it can be ignored that inflation, including that of food, was an obvious, predicted consequence of locking down most of the planet for a respiratory virus.

It's not just the West, of course. The bewilderingly mad Chinese zero COVID policy has gone a long way to snapping supply chains for good. Why, oh why, have they done this? Locking down Shanghai so hard for so long was so utterly, blatantly destructive whilst providing negligible benefits. There simply must be ulterior motives.

I daren't wade into arcane Chinese politics but what IS going on?! Is Xi seeking to encourage more global inflation to break the monetary system? The line I get from my Hong Kong friend is that it's all to do with "face". Having brain-farted something about China's amazing zero COVID policy, Xi is unable to back down and appear to have contradicted himself.

Really? It seems like the easiest thing to do, once everyone had decided to label Omicron cold-alike, is to change tack on the basis that the facts have changed. Would a bit of PR and scientific fluff of having braved the dangerous variants really been worse than starving and mentally torturing a city of 25 million people? People the whole World can then watch losing their minds on TikTok?

Anyway, it will be the poorest at the margin who will suffer first and most. *Peter Ziehan's* book, *Disunited Nations* interestingly set out the nations that he thought were most self-reliant when it comes to food and energy. Clearly, there are worse places to be than Australia (from where I am writing this) but even here the economy is built on a narrative underpinning house prices that resemble the arse end of a game of Jenga.

Most of the West has already been eating processed, industrial filth for the last few decades. Shortages of food globally will presumably see even more of our poor children being fed canned or packaged foodstuffs.

But it will be difficult to have sympathy left over for the West's bloated, diabetic teenagers when those currently living subsistence lifestyles start running out of the basics.

Already, we have seen riots in Peru and Sri Lanka (now also running out of medicines). These apparently peripheral developments are kept out of the MSM headlines in favour of parochial party politics and poorly behaving celebrities.

4) Plague

No. Ner-no. While it has been the crazed reaction to COVID that has gone a long way to setting the World on this hideously turbulent path - whether by devilish design or by cowardly, lockstep groupthink – that was never the real plague.

As John Ioannidis, the Stanford University professor specialising in epidemiology and one of the most published and influential scientists in the World, pointed out at the very beginning of the shamdemic, the

Infection Fatality Rate of the 'Rona was likely to be close to that of a bad flu. Subsequent data bears that out. And that is in an environment where re-purposed therapeutics were outlawed – where doctors were prevented from treating patients until they were hospital-bound.

So, no. The real plague is that of misplaced fear and how it has leached through the pores of the myriad mainstream and social media outlets.

Already we are talking about Monkeypox as the next threat. I am reading that the EU wants to target the unvaxxed for their (2022) autumn program of boosters (for WHAT?!).

Whoever genuinely thinks that the escalation in fear over climate change is a natural amplification of concerns in line with empirical or scientific evidence, then I suspect that they will not have made it this far into this book.

We are simply too early in the on-line media revolution to grasp how we are reacting. Or being manipulated. It took hundreds of years and a preponderance of vile (literal) witch hunts for the impacts of the printing press to settle into an equilibrium. The shock to the learned classes of having information so radically democratised caused intense harms in the short run before then leading to The Enlightenment and the greatest leaps forward in progress in human history.

The real plague has been that of unwarranted and misdirected fear.

Except that plagues are normally as a result of exogenous biological forces.

5) Lack of Good Roads

For ancient roads read modern supply chains.

The intriguingly persistent, multi-decade marketing campaign for renewables has consequentially cut short supply chains for energy. Low density energy harvested intermittently from solar and wind farms cannot be economically transported long distances. The more we rely on these sources of energy, the more inflexible and expensive our energy becomes. The proposed "electrification" of our energy grids intrinsically constrains communities from thriving away from energy-generating hubs or expensive and resource-intensive infrastructure.

Over-egged renewables policies have driven an over-reliance on fewer external parties for baseload oil and gas, weaponizing energy. As a result, Russia had already restricted flows of oil and gas to Europe before the "sabotage" of Nordstream – an event astonishingly downplayed (again) in the MSM when it could prove to be in the same league of geopolitical importance as 9/11. Broken and stunted supply chains for fossil fuels are likely to cost us dear.

More recently, COVID policies had already caused colossal bottlenecks for physical goods at ports all over the World, including the major US ports. Clearly, the Chinese zero COVID policies have obliterated supply chains relying on Shanghai and Tianjin. This also caused shipping rates to reach and maintain record levels.

Chains of goods have been broken and will never return to the nature, size and efficiency that they previously saw. People will, for the foreseeable future, price in and weigh up security of supply against the fair-weather cost. Political necessity and roboticization will see countries manufacturing a far broader range of products and component parts within their own borders, albeit at what will initially be a higher cost.

That transition will add to inflation and the general costs of living. I suspect it will be extraordinary painful for the very many who had grown used to comfortable and secure lives.

For many on the precipice of poverty, I fear it will be fatal.

Looking further into the future, those retracted supply chains will lead to less sharing of information and ideas. Less innovation. Fewer solutions for the alleviation of human and environmental suffering.

[And relax]

Well…poor little Raf didn't have to suffer all of that rant in one go!

But, I do think there is an argument that we have found ourselves catapulting into hurricane headwinds at least as challenging as those that brought down the Roman Empire and ushered in the Dark Ages.

Just imagine if tomorrow the electricity, the wifi, the water was turned off…that supermarkets, petrol stations were empty…that paper money was valued only for its physical substance. Suddenly, computers, phones, cars also become next to useless.

How many of us would know how to find and provide the very basics of human life: water, food, clothing and shelter. With no tools. Just the physical, natural World around us and our own ingenuity.

How soon before we end up as Dark Age, nit-infested scavengers marvelling at the monuments to human achievement around us…tower blocks based on technological expertise so dispersed no one person could possibly combine the required skills without the digital wiring upon which our modern World so heavily relies.

Back to Basics

The next stop on our World Detour was an idyllic farmhouse deep in the Pyrenees. Coll de Nargo.

After much guilt-tinged deliberating about the chunky cost, we had reasoned that we were on a once in a lifetime educational adventure as a family and, armed with these righteous justifications, paid a fortune for five days in a three-story 11th century farmhouse. It had a (somewhat chilly) pool but otherwise was largely a throwback to foregone centuries. Grapes grew in the garden, the floors groaned wearily under each step and the heavy timber doors carried iron latches that required a shoulder-shove to shift. The farmhouse even had its own chapel.

Yeeeeees, Rex found it a little scary. But we soon found ourselves used to living there. I surprised myself by being completely sanguine about night-time bats flying in and out of my bedroom. It was a sublime environment in which to de-clutter ourselves.

This was a wonderfully soothing reminder of how simple life could be. And how a simple life could be so enriching.

A mutually helpful mini eco-system where all the basics were produced locally, in tune with the seasons. You don't *need* Peruvian asparagus in August. You don't *need* kiwi flown in from tropical climes.

Tomatoes, cucumber, lettuce, some cheese and some meat. And, it goes without saying, a splash of the local wine. Some padron peppers. A homemade pizza.

All that and much more without relying on the World beyond a 50-mile radius.

If things really do start going wobbly, I wonder how much more resilient trusting, inter-reliant communities like Coll de Nargo will be compared to the faceless, brand-obsessed cities.

Hopefully, we will not find out.

Anyway, our family was lucky enough to be able to live in this farmhouse for a cathartically rural week. Within earshot of the permanently chattering river but beyond that of any other human existence, our home for the week afforded the constant luxury of living with one's own thoughts.

We ate, we stretched, we stargazed on the roof terrace each night. Shooting stars proved to be more of a regular feature of the night sky than I had been led to believe.

And it warmed my heart that Raf always wanted to join me under the stars. Not speaking much. Just the occasional comment. There is always something to say, a question to muse, when ogling the universe and allowing your thoughts to dissipate into the starry oblivion.

Like a truly loving father, I marched manfully through as many beers as was humanly possible, so as to provide the metal missiles for their sword fights in the garden. We had created a game whereby we would throw volleys of empty cans at each of Rex and Raf as they flicked their wooden swords (from Olite) back and forth to defend themselves from the flurry of incoming tins.

Like Yoda teaching Luke Skywalker to sense the force.

Only with wooden swords. And beer cans.

It was at this stage that we, as a family, were hitting peak World Detour relaxation. We had chalked up enough of the destination experiences to start properly enjoying just being in Spain. And not yet having to worry about leaving.

To stop thinking about what to do next and just enjoy being there.

The days were filled with long, meandering discussions about which Greek god each of us would like to be and why. Or reading in one of the multitude of different nooks and crannies hidden in the stone homestead.

Time spent cooking was time indulged. Not rushed or for a purpose. Time relished.

Raf and I even fermented our own homemade wine with a collection of grapes from the garden. After a week of the most basic vintnering, I have to say that the results surpassed my more extreme hopes (not that I drank more than a sip!).

Disappointingly, I couldn't resist connecting with the on-line madness. Surges in my blood pressure caused by regular updates of what was happening on Planet Earth, beyond our patch of pressure-free paradise, would act as a constant reminder that we were living in a temporary state of detachment.

Australia, at this stage, was going astonishingly nuts! Kim Yong Dan, in Melbourne, was openly threatening the "un-vaxxed" with being excluded from everyday society. His "police" were firing rubber bullets at their own people. For their health. Gladystopia, in Sydney, was pulling an extra 500 "police" onto the streets of Sydney to enforce extremist communist lockdown measures.

Sitting there in the mountain tranquillity, the hypnotic rushing of the river undergirding a permanent timelessness, it was instructive to take a step back and register how holding a screen in front of your face – whilst sat in that landscape – could bring all the worst troubles on the face of the Earth to the very forefront of your consciousness.

From mindfulness to mindlessness.

Painful Departure

As I think so many of us do on our holidays (telling in itself), we fantasised about creating ourselves a simpler, more honest lifestyle in Coll de Nargo. How wonderfully cleansing it would be to switch everything off and concentrate on day-to-day living through the seasons.

But, of course, there was another societal guard rail that ushered us away from such reveries – schooling for the children.

The question of what to do about schooling for the Boys had been an on-going debate. Of course, we knew to be sceptical of how the lunacy in Australia was being amplified. However, it was impossible to ignore video evidence of gun-happy riot police and junkie-eyed state premiers (that Northern Territories Gunner chap was either on acid or scared out of his wits) frothing at the mouth as they eviscerate the unvaxxed.

Ultimately, the borders were closed.

So, Kate and I had to rethink our previously intended Antipodean arrival date of October. It did not look as if schools there would be open by that time, in any case.

We talked genuinely, if quixotically, about renting somewhere in Spain for the winter and finding an international school in Gerona. How amazing would that be for the Boys' life education and how motivating for Kate and I would it be to have to make a go of it under such sink-or-swim pressure?

However, as we assessed the more detailed practicalities of taking a spontaneous decision, enough of the realities emerged to make it clear to us that we should pull back to a path closer to the beaten track.

And through those discussions, we reached a conclusion that we should spend the rest of 2021 in the UK countryside, in my hometown of Shrewsbury in Shropshire. And that the Boys, if at all possible, should spend at least a term at my old prep school, Prestfelde.

Whilst these decisions were the logical outputs from the questions Kate and I were facing, they took us all by complete surprise. It took a fair bit of re-jigging of the synapses to compute what the next, unscheduled leg of our World Detour would look like.

At the age of 48 and on the cusp of being unemployed, my family and I would be living with my mother as we asked the Boys to readjust from our España escapade to a British prep school that I had last visited in the early 1980s.

And thus, it came to be. I swapped some obsequious emails with the admissions lady at the school (leaning heavily on my rose-tinted memories) who was incredibly accommodating and lovely. After some fiddly form-filling, we had enough of a thumbs-up to be sure that this was the new plan.

Roses

It was with a regretful longing that we departed Coll de Nargo and headed back to the coast for our goodbye-to-Spain leg. As the summer had worn on and World Detour increasingly clashed with the holidays of the locals, our choices had narrowed for this last week before heading to the UK.

Nevertheless, we managed to stumble upon another gem, a place called Roses. For our last week in the Mediterranean sun, we would be perched overlooking a 500m beach that sunbathed contentedly next to the ancient sapphire waters.

Roses was much more of a mainstream tourist venue than El Port de la Selva. The beach would fill up quickly in the morning and the hum of motorboats and jet skis formed the audio backdrop of a more traditional family summer holiday. Looking down on the beach at Roses, it felt like a time and place to make the transition from a immersive, meditative experience of Spain to that of looking back on the adventures we had so enjoyed together, whilst at the same time starting to set our attention to the challenges and uncertainties ahead.

That said, we still loved it. We had a long, wooden dining table outside, surveying the ever-changing bikini- and swimmer-clad personnel on the sands below. We interspersed our homemade feasts with trips to the next-door restaurant which offered a superb selection of fresh fish.

And my indulgence in Mediterranean history was not over just yet. Not a long drive away was Sant Marti d'Empuries and its ancient Greco-Roman town.

Just phenomenal. These wonderfully preserved and detailed ruins on the shore of the Mediterranean provided another window into the daily lives of the past. Once again, the perennial dashing of the tide on the nearby rocks provided a cushioning soundtrack that has remained uninterrupted for millennia.

I allowed myself to get completely carried away, gushing in front of Rex and Raf about the articulate debates that would filled the palisaded forum, the pungent aromas that would have hung heavily in market square - herbs, spices, dried fish.

With our imaginations stoked and senses piqued, we headed back to the Roses beach for a farewell dinner.

Everything about our last night in Roses was rose. The venue, the wine and, with splendid symbolism, the sensational sunset.

The next morning would see a clinical team-scurry to clean our accommodation, pack the car and head off to the airport.

But for a glorious, final evening on the Med, on the terrace of our next-door fish restaurant, it was time to let the warmth of the dimming sun flow over us, to shine a flush-pink glow over our family, our thoughts and our senses.

Adios, España.

PART III - LATE TRANSITION
The United Kingdom

"Home is where the heart is"

Pliny the Elder

UK AOK

It had been a pining goodbye to a wonderful, culture-blessed country that we truly love. However, if there was one place on the planet to which I could have travelled next for a soft landing, it would have been England.

We had again invested a fair amount of time and mental energy in sorting out our travel paperwork. In Roses, we had popped into the local doctor to perform a rapid lateral flow test. It is no exaggeration that it was the receptionist who carried out the test in five minutes. She simply typed our passport details into a standard template with a formal letterhead sporting the practice's name and address. EUR 50. Cash only. Just a pointless process. A racket.

But it did the job required and we are able to have a cheerful chinwag with the jovial customs chappy as we smoothly swanned through immigration control and transitioned to the next stage of our World Detour.

The cold, wet, Brummy-accented familiarity wrapped around us as we emerged through the arrivals gate, providing an immediate breath of fresh air. As we clattered and crammed our bulging cases into the cab, it was with to a backdrop of English advertising boards, passing slang conversations, yellow number plates and jokey radio.

England has always been my home. And it was good to be back.

It's a strange sensation, coming back to your home country after having made a life - a daily household - elsewhere for seven years. Returning to the place where you turned from child to teenager to adult but after having adapted to an entirely different culture and environment. For seven years I had led a life parallel to the one that had presented itself as the obvious path. For Rex and Raf that seven years constituted their whole lives. For them this was a holiday novelty. For me the surroundings bore a reminiscence of another life story. A storyline from which I had departed. The hedgerows, the trees…the no nonsense chat from the taxi driver. I most definitely sensed affection, affiliation and attachment… but distinctly less of belonging. It sounds obvious, but here was the physical manifestation of a part of the World that had been getting on with its life without me. The place that I called home had moved on.

I found myself a little disorientated as to why I found that somewhat… stark.

An enjoyable and chatty 1½ -hour ride through the fresh countryside found us drawing up outside my mother's house. Cricket and weather were dominant topics en route and we all studiously steered clear of the C-discussion. No need to stride into the conversational hornets' nest just yet.

Arriving home…to my family home, my mother's home…felt like plugging back into the mains when one's battery is running uncomfortably low. The Boys, excited so see their grandmother ("Omi", as they call her) again, were beautifully generous with their hugs. As is her time-honoured routine on such occasions, Mum cracked open the champagne and we provided a precis of our adventures since we had parted ways in Tarragona.

I should have mentioned: this was a Thursday evening. The Friday was Rex's birthday. And the Monday would see both Raf's birthday and the Boys' first day at a traditional English prep school! So, there was going to be a flurry of "moments" coming our way over the ensuing days. I made some minor preparations by putting up some celebratory decorations in the kitchen before heading to bed.

New Terms

One massive plus was the unusually glorious, sunny September weather. It meant that we could spend hours and hours of those first few days playing cricket or football, reading and chatting in Mum's stunning garden. Whilst a vast amount of work and tenderness had been poured into nursing her flowerbeds and lawn, Mum was surprisingly relaxed about one of the Boys hoiking a long hop into a rose bud or the other etching an earthy groove into the immaculately bladed carpet with a reckless sliding tackle.

I cannot recall the patchwork of if/and/or/whether rules that were then in place, but the conclusion had been that Kate and I had to self-isolate at home whilst Rex, Raf and Mum were fine to do as they wished.

As required by the UK's officious cretins, Kate and I had spent hundreds of pounds on numerous Randox lateral flow tests to be sent in the post over the following days in order to comply with government requirements.

But Rex, on his 9th birthday, was merrily oblivious and was wired all day. We couldn't have visitors. A party was impossible. As was any birthday treat excursion. But he was just so happy for it being his special day, finding his heavily trailed Avengers lego set and, crucially, being lavished with positive responses to requests for more cake, snacks and juices.

However, over that weekend, as Kate and I could not leave the grounds of our designated address, my dearest mother had to set about gathering items required under the bewildering school uniform list. I had tried to forewarn Kate about the insanely over-complicated nature of prep school uniform requirements, but the true extent only dawned over that weekend. Mum had to queue, with a lot of pain in her foot from a tenacious corn, in line with feverishly stressed families in the pre-term, last-minute scramble for overpriced school socks.

Monday came and my heart glowed with pride as Raf first celebrated his 7th birthday with a morning cuddle in our bed but then pragmatically donned his emergency school uniform and set about heading to school. Rex was equally positive and it was with a sense of grateful relief that we saw them happily trot off to their first day at a new school with their Omi.

I don't know about you, but I am still prone to occasional school flashbacks and corresponding bouts of anxiety. I am not sure if our two young men are just more resilient than me or whether there were more emotions bubbling under the surface than they were letting on, but I was just so impressed with their "get on with it" approach. They strode into a school they had never seen before with a bunch of British kids of whom they knew not one.

Mum, Kate and I still had plenty of admin to keep us occupied as we excitedly, nosily awaited their review of the first day at a new school.

Thoughtfully, to colour in those monotonous moments in between prep school prepping, I set about exploring with Mum a layer deeper than we had previously roamed on the whole COVID question. Eager to discover the lay of the land in COVID terms, I set about canvassing her perspective. Poor Mum!

I was interested to find out that she was pretty relaxed on the "rules". She had friends that were complete sticklers and others that were half calling bullshit. Having a very active and broad social life (at least outside of lockdowns) Mum had to navigate a range of views in order to maintain the activities and interactions which she so enjoyed.

On the questions of "vaccines", she was much more definitive. She believed that they were "safe and effective". She did not know that the "vaccines" were only under EUA. Nor had she heard anything about adverse events. The terms VAERS and Yellow Card were not familiar to her.

My Mum

Everything about my mother is golden. She has a warm sunny disposition, empathetic and welcoming. Despite elegantly gliding into her 80s, her hair has never shone any colour other than blond.

But most of all, she has a heart of gold. She is kind. She finds an energy in helping others and thrives on creating happiness.

It's a natural, if not necessary, side effect of such a personality to worry about what others think. And my mother really does care what others think.

And this is where the mind games played by those orchestrating these psychologically manipulative messages (SAGE, yes, but MSM and others too) are just so filthily pernicious:

- I am very confident of my position and feel it a moral duty to challenge what I sincerely believe are deeply immoral, unethical laws and regulations;
- However, doing so without moderation could negatively impact my mother and her close-knit social life.

Essentially, once you have a critical mass of people who are convinced that there is only one right and decent way for people to behave, anyone challenging that belief or not adhering to that misplaced conformity, ends up socially (not physically) damaging those that they love.

The loved ones may fully respect the non-conforming views and be open to mutually beneficial discussion and debate. But the loved one cannot separate themselves from the externally viewed "Covidiot" taint of being close to someone who dissents.

This mismatch first presented itself with the clown show that was the testing procedures. Having registered the Randox tests on-line, I missed a call from "test-and-trace". Mum was worried that, as a result of missing a phone call, the police would come around...and maybe the neighbours would see the police coming around.

I felt like an insensitive hooligan son who had come home to trash his mother's peaceful way of life.

They really fucked with us. They really did. This is why less government is always the better option. We are better at sorting out matters amongst ourselves. The sheer idiocy of the concept that we need a remote, external organisation to instruct communities on how best to work for each other is well summed-up by *Thomas Sowell:*

"It is hard to imagine a more stupid or more dangerous way of making decisions than by putting those decisions in the hands of people who pay no price for being wrong."

Anyway, the (genuinely) lovely lady from test-and-trace called a second time and asked if I was OK with them sharing my information with "the Home Office and others". I asked who the "others" might be and she suggested (as she did not know) that I read the UK government's COVID privacy page.

From what I could gather through a substantial stint of forensic internet sleuthing via a complex, snaking trail of references and links, agreeing to that request would allow the Home Office to sequence my genome and share it with whomever they deem it beneficial for the furtherment of non-defined goals.

That sounds like conspiratorial craziness, I know. But take a look!

Thankfully, no-one ever phoned back.

In the background, Australian state premiers were ever more forcefully "othering" the non-vaxxed. An astonishing violation of ethics. The epitome of the valueless, self-aggrandising elite, Christine Lagarde, stated on camera that we must "vaccinate" the whole World.

With a "vaccine" under EUA. And no long-term safety data.

Just. Think. About that.

Please.

Settling into Shrewsbury

A striking new experience for Kate and I was us both having the weekdays wholly free and to ourselves, from drop-off to pick-up. Huge, potentially productive chunks of time with which to do as we saw fit.

Of course, it wasn't all plain sailing. Rex had a harder time slotting into school as, in his year, he was experiencing a multiple whammy. Had we stayed in Hong King, he would automatically have had to adjust to attending the senior school with its more rigid daily routines. Lessons, bells, subjects. But in this case, those schooling step changes were coming packaged alongside a new school in a new country. He was confronted with this one-hit readjustment alongside playing football in the rain, wearing an over-sized blazer, different classes for different lessons, etc.

In retrospect, he did unbelievably well to have only one wobble when he refused to go to school one day – he stayed at home and just read. After that one day, he quickly cottoned on to the fact that football was a key "in" for being part of the group, being one of the boys. For fitting in.

My goodness, I cringe as I write that now.

Let me re-phrase that: Rex quickly worked out the qualities that were most respected by his peers and set about improving his abilities in that realm. And he did so successfully. Football became a core part of what school was about and we loved watching him play with his new friends and teamies. Kate and I would double-up laughing after catching ourselves being completely caught up in key moments of action.

Involuntary yelps and jerking of clenched limbs would accompany a goal mouth ping-pong. Kate, more than once, let slip a high-pitched expletive and I found myself as nervous as I can remember being watching football since the 1990 Word Cup!

The boys were also hilarious in how they studied, rehearsed and then performed their goal celebrations. Ronaldo (predictably) was the most emulated.

Raf, on the other hand, found it immensely frustrating that he was deemed too young to be able to play football! Gratingly, the school also had some strange (health and safety?) policies preventing younger kids from playing in the same areas as the older ones. It was against the rules for Raf to play with his older brother when their breaks overlapped.

Kate and I railed against this confected nonsense of segregating kids by year groups. We firmly believe it is hugely beneficial for older and younger kids to learn from and teach each other.

But Raf was like a duck to water. He made friends, enchanted his teacher and loved being his rumbunctious self.

Kate and I were brimming with pride about how the Boys had approached and dealt with the daunting process of finding their way in a new school.

I wondered if they will have school flashbacks.

Medieval Discovery

Kate and I had not thought to plan what to do with the luxurious stretches of time suddenly afforded to us. Two or three weeks beforehand, there had been no intention to send the Boys to school in England and we had been so busy entangled in cross-border COVID paperwork, logistics and school prepping that these indulgent personal feasts came at us out of the blue.

We both found it simultaneously intriguing and inspiring that we enjoyed each other's company enough to spend a lot of time together.

We would either make the 15-minute stroll into town together or arrange to meet up for a coffee mid-morning. In addition to the cafés, Shrewsbury presented an unusually broad array of charity shops in which we could justifiably splurge, given our sparse baggage that had accompanied us since Hong Kong had never been selected to accommodate an English autumn or winter.

There was also a ridiculously addictive Oxfam bookshop where we found ourselves justifying one another's purchases on the basis that we had to build up a base library in our temporary home.

The inside of arguably the ugliest building in Shrewsbury, The Market, belied its 1960s brick block exterior and swiftly became our favourite venue. A lovely, overly generous man ran a stall selling second hand Beano and Dandy comics. Amazing fresh veg, meats and fish was one sale alongside Airfix models, local arts and crafts, including craft gin. Crucially, The Market also housed a couple of fantastic lunch spots that were to become our regular go-to eateries. One was Thai, the other an Asian dumpling shop.

If we had done our own pottering before meeting, Kate and I would meet there to catch each other up on items under consideration as well as any stand-out snippets from the podcasts that had accompanied our strolls.

In the early days, Kate and I had sat around brainstorming ideas for how to recreate ourselves post leaving Hong Kong. These enormously enjoyable sessions would see us scribble out mental drawing boards with genuinely valuable ideas. Ideas not entirely lapsed.

As we all know, it is by our actions not our words that we are ultimately judged...and, as of writing, those actions still need to be realised.

Friends Reunited

Shrewsbury is my hometown. I lived there from the age of five until leaving for university. And I was excited about reacquainting myself with its many attributes. Being a medieval market town, Shrewsbury boasts a treasure trove of history but also theatre, a splendid array of Olde Worlde pubs and a meandering river that picturesquely snakes into the surrounding fields. But it also provided an opportunity to reconnect with time-honoured friends.

I knew that the hot topic of COVID would be front and centre but, having seen such an array of takes from Hong Kong across Asia Pacific and then in Spain, I hoped that an overarching live and let live approach had won the day. It was with small steps that I ventured out on eggshells as the topic inevitably came up.

If any of my friends veered from the mainstream Sky News line, it was to an imperceptible degree. A lot were grateful to Lockdown for providing the additional time to spend with family, not having to commute, saving money.

For one of my friends, when we met over a beer, it was his first visit to a pub for two over years...and he said he hadn't missed it.

People were just beginning to meet up more regularly, but it was with some trepidation, even reluctance.

It did help that, while we were there, the 'Rona was starting to explode. It was ripping through schools and friend groups. It was certainly no longer an exceptional or extraordinary confession to admit that you had tested positive for the virus.

As time went on, more people had it. Most people knew someone who had had it.

And nearly no-one knew anyone who had been seriously ill with it.

And then we all caught it.

'Rona

I think it was as a result of a request to test from the school, that was seeing swathes of its pupils and then parents test positive for COVID, that Raf tested positive on a lateral flow test. It was a Sunday afternoon and we had just started watching the Grand Prix. From the sofa we managed to book a slot for a PCR test, stroll there and get back in time to see Lewis Hamilton win the race.

The PCR result was also positive and this news set in motion what was to be 15 days of a variety of experiences in Mum's home:

- Mum – double vaxxed and very recently boosted, she suffered the symptoms of a severe cold;
- Kate – heavily fatigued and bed-ridden for a couple of days. Lost sense of smell;
- Myself – felt sluggish with cold symptoms;
- Rex – took nearly ten days after Raf to test positive, but then a bit coldy;
- Raf – zero impact. Running around like a maniac throughout.

I am going to struggle to set this out without talking my own book, spinning it the way I wanted it to be, but I will do my very best to be as objective as possible.

Kate was hit the hardest by both COVID and her family's pent-up reaction to her not taking the "vaccine". A significant portion of the first day after her testing positive was spent on FaceTime with a variety of family members.

It was very interesting for me to hear what they had to say. It was almost as if they had learnt the exam answers. And they were essentially the exact same phrases and soundbites as those we had heard in the UK. Obviously, Kate's family had not sat down and revised the arguments, but it was obvious to me that through repetition, be it by written, audio or televised press, they had absorbed these as the "scientific" responses to each of our deviations from the narrative. In particular, there was the line that critical care wards were filling up (in Australia) and that this was a "pandemic of the unvaccinated". At the time – October 2021 – it was just starting to become palpably undeniable that these "vaccines" didn't stop infection or transmission, but it was not yet possible to show just how poor their performance was going to be.

It may have been that Kate was thinking, in for a penny in for a pound, when she told her veterinarian father that she was taking Ivermectin (we had secured some in Hong Kong before we left). This sent my father-in-law into paroxysms and he genuinely came out with the view that its efficacy was part of a right-wing conspiracy theory. I don't remember him actually calling Ivermectin horse-dewormer...but it felt as if he had.

I set about frantically typing the counter-arguments / logic for the danger of mass inoculating such huge proportions of our populations with an experimental "vaccine" in the midst of a purported pandemic. I never sent it. But it felt therapeutic for me to write it.

Kate also suffered the worst symptoms from out of the five of us in the household. She was bedridden for two/three days and there was one night when she was concerned about her breathing. She mused over whether that concern was borne of the concept being at the forefront of her mind. Would it have occurred to her that she might be short of breath if the media had not been dramatizing patients on ventilators and pushing the lurid testimonies of those that were suffering or had suffered breathlessness to the forefront of our consciousness? Who knows.

Anyway, she was on the mend and suffering more from the forced self-isolation than the bug by the end of four days.

Where I struggled most was on the subject of Mum's and my reaction to the virus – but not its physical effects. Mum didn't test positive until about a week after Raf, almost at the same time as Kate. And she had the equivalent of a bad winter cold…bordering on flu, if you were to ask her to self-diagnose.

But it generated this awful unspoken tension.

I don't think it is credible to deny the fact that my bringing our young, school-going family into her home increased the chances of her catching COVID earlier. And that her getting COVID increased the chances of her being ill or even seriously ill.

My strong belief was that these incremental risks were small. I knew for a fact that Mum thought they were considerably larger. For very understandable reasons.

At the same time, I was fully aware of what the accepted narrative was: Granny Killer.

Of course, I couldn't stop my mind and, yes, my conscience from exploring worst case scenarios and how those might play out…how they might feel. What it would mean for the rest of my life and, by extension, that of the Boys.

These terrible thoughts were my personal projections, but Mum must have explored her own worst-case scenarios. And it simply cannot have been the case that she did not also consume the Granny Killer narrative but from a far more vulnerable perspective.

It saddens me that we were not able to confront these feelings and mind-generated anxieties. Naturally, at such times, we are wired to worry and crash test possible outcomes and the best way of pulling these concerns back into perspective is always connecting and communicating with people.

But that we failed to do.

Whether it was due to an underlying sense of guilt that I harboured or a resentment on behalf of Mum, I felt as if I was to blame for putting Mum in a life-threatening position.

The fact that the "vaccine" does not prevent (or even mitigate?) transmission, the fact that she would have caught the virus at some stage anyway, the fact that she was as protected as she ever could be… none of that really mattered.

Somehow, instead of supporting each other, we allowed this unspoken idea to pervade the atmosphere - that I would be deemed to be an anti vaxx, granny-killing covidiot.

They really fucked with us. They really did.

My own COVID bout was rather muted compared to Kate's. About the same as Mum's. I had a mild temperature one night but other than that, experienced normal-ish, cold-like symptoms. What differed was a sluggishness. I found it hard to concentrate on reading a book (I had just finished one and had a couple of false starts on new books). I even found it hard to listen to podcasts (VERY unusual!). It wasn't until Kate pointed out that she had lost her sense of smell that I realised I had also lost mine. I delved around in our spice rack inhaling turmeric, cumin and…chilli. Nada!

That was the only great differentiating factor. Pre the hypochondriac hysteria of the last year and a half, I would not have thought twice about going into work in the state that I was in. I had endured days in the office in a far worse condition (I am stupidly proud of my record of only ever having had one sick day in my 27-year career).

Just think of all those lovely sofa days that I would have enjoyed under the "new normal" of pulling a sickie at the drop of a handkerchief.

Rex and Raf were just themselves. If anything, Raf was more energetic and precocious than usual but that might just have been our perception viewed through a lens of knowing we could not take him out and about for an energy-dissipating run around the block.

In the end, as a family, we didn't quite make it to the end of our designated isolation period. On the Saturday, 13 days after Raf first tested positive, we headed out to the Shropshire hills. It was one of those English days with low, slowly skudding clouds where it feels as if you are still in a room. But we had a lovely stroll in the expansive Great Outdoors. From separate vantage points, Kate and I watched R&R act out another sword fight, albeit in Medieval Britain rather than Crusader Spain.

Happily, we did convene a "clear the air" roundtable with Mum. And to be fair, Kate and I had been avoiding making hard and fast plans. As a broad, overriding desire, we wanted to pitch camp in our lovely Montville home, get the Lads up and running at school and in sports and to start building our new lives. But goddamit – these authority-addled politicians all over the planet were coming out with irrational abject nonsense and it was incredibly difficult to predict what we would be able to do where and when.

The meeting certainly helped give Mum a better idea of what we were thinking and also helped us firm up a working plan. It was understood that it was a schedule that would be adapted to the whims of rule makers at various points along our intended path.

We were aiming to be ensconced on the Sunshine Coast by the end of January (beginning of the Australian school year) having snuck in a visit to our Russian friends from Hong Kong who were now adjusting to a life in Dubai.

However, we as a family, had another minor detour to make before that plan could be hoped to run its path.

Croatia

It is a painfully contorted explanation but, in order not to put my deferred bonus at risk I had to a) keep working until pay day at the end of October; and b) until then, be seen to be heading back to Hong Kong to resume my alter ego.

The latter requirement saw me head out to Croatia as soon as I could be confident of not testing positive on the lateral flow test needed to get out there.

So, a few days after emerging from our COVID experiences, I flew to Split.

It felt timely…a genuine reason for giving my mother some space.

Kate, Rex and Raf. I utterly adore my family. I miss them with a passion when I am away from them. I had the warm comfort of knowing that they would be joining me in a few days' time. But I can't lie…there are times when I quite enjoy my own company. And I enjoyed my pokey Split bedsit (EUR 50 a night on AirBnB) enormously. I had a promptly-filled fridge of very drinkable Croatian lager, an OKish bed and a load of books to read. I enjoyed a random collection of:

- The Molecule of More (podcast recommendation about dopamine);

- Wild Swans (a reflective goodbye to Hong Kong); and
- and a Jeffrey Archer novel, Only Time Will Tell (a guilty pleasure – I find him "unputdownable"!).

I spent hours on the sunny balcony on the 8th floor overlooking the rest of the housing estate.

By this stage, I was officially "working from abroad" and so had to be logged onto the bank's IT system and essentially monitor emails. Knowing that I was less than a week away from handing in my notice, I was spectacularly unmotivated. However, it did thoroughly reassure me that I now had life goals that differed from those of my colleagues. As I Skyped around my team, after three months of being totally off-line for what they understood to be a career break, for two of them the main line of re-engagement was to start pushing hard for pay increases. In our first calls together after a quarter of a year.

Had my mind been re-wired from thinking about what is true wealth… versus being (fiat) monetarily rich? The result of a podcast echo chamber (albeit one that echoes back millennia)? Was it a case of me self-soothing my concerns about walking away from such a remunerative career? Or simply that I was spoilt in having built a platform that conveyed the financial security required for a mid-life crisis?

Whichever, I felt a sense of detached disinterest. I did not value that for which they were desperate for me to fight. So how could I fight for it to the best of my ability?

I just could not devote my energy, my time…my *life*…to those goals anymore. I didn't want to be part of it.

Definitely, time for me to pass on the team reins to someone more aligned.

I enjoyed telling my Australian colleague that I had taken Ivermectin (I think Australia has suffered the most savage propaganda campaign on this particular component of the COVID calamity).

For what it's worth, 2021 ended up being a bumper year for the financial sector. Whilst the seeds of mass poverty and famine were ruthlessly strewn across the developing countries…whilst the elderly were slipping away from this life in clinical hospital beds absent the warm grip - a kiss - from their family, banks were making out like bandits.

The head of our investment bank even stated to the press that this was going to be a fantastic year for bonuses before having to wind his neck in, due to the blowback of public revulsion.

However, 2021 did indeed prove to be a record year for bonuses. The first year in which I would not partake of the annual feeding frenzy. About which I felt remarkably sanguine.

The volume of work was thankfully slow and so I was able sit out on the balcony-for-one with a book or a podcast liberally dosing myself with solar Vitamin D (sunbathing).

This solo time also led to the initiation of what has been an epic, rolling WhatsApp debate with one of my very best friends. A super-bright, tenacious debater we have been locking horns on whatever topic we could find since puberty.

Pub Chat

My friend and I were amongst the group of "lads" at school that first made it to the pub. I cannot think of what was the driving force that caused us to seek out sitting in a smoky room drinking alcohol, in breach of the law, in our early teens. However, in Shrewsbury in the late 1980s it was possible to get served with a pint of beer in selected hostelries from about the age of about 14.

We soon got to know which ones took a more relaxed approach to licensing laws.

And we would sit there, with our outsized glass of ale, and talk.

Sometimes, we would be eagerly chatting on the way into the pub, impatiently holding on to our train of thought whilst the beers were being served.

Other times, we would have to enjoy the effects of a draught, or sometimes two, in relative silence before the flow of conversation took over and led us into realms of virgin thought.

But conversationally comradery-building it always was. And still is.

Anyway, I mention the WhatsApp debate as it has become an excellent log (in my view) of arguments on both sides. I genuinely think the substance of our disagreement and the manner in which we held the discussion is on a higher level than anything I have seen on any media.

I have read and researched strong and powerful arguments put forward from either side of the divide on COVID restrictions and "vaccine" mandates. However, I have not seen an open dialogue. A debate. A mutual challenging of positions. And I am deeply grateful to have had it.

Hurrah for Hvar

When was the last time you had a weekend city break on your own?

This is, in essence, what lay before me in Split. And it was awesome. The Saturday saw me laze around the historic old town, ducking into museums and markets, strolling up the surrounding hills and dithering over at which of the plethora of establishments to exchange my appetite for a belly load of local meats. As the sun eased its way under the

Adriatic horizon, I flip-flopped down to the ferry terminal to plan my Sunday trip to the island of Hvar.

Hvar was a secluded island of calm. Crystal waters beckoned the sun's bright rays from the cobalt blue sky to pierce deep under the surface, revealing pristine rocks strewn across the contoured seabed. It felt timeless.

Even in such a precious, unique set of circumstances – a day, an island, an unexplored local history all to myself – the German gene kicked in! I still needed to earn the indulgent meal that I had mentally lined up. And so I walked for hours. I tracked the coastline south as far as the pathway would allow. I trekked up the island's highest hill to the castle with its accessible dungeon cells – an insight into the wasted lives that slowly deteriorated locked in stone.

Having then explored as far north as easy passage would admit, I had the perfect amount of time to allocate to my octopus salad and charcoal-grilled vegetables before heading back to the port for my ferry trip back to the mainland.

Relieved to be back in the bedsit cocoon, I FaceTimed the family and heard the galling news that my niece had tested PCR positive for COVID. Galling, not because she was at any risk of being ill, but because it meant that my sister and her family would have to call off their enormously valued half-term holiday to Valencia.

Having spent the day languidly wondering the ancient Dalmation shores of Hvar, lost in my meditative musings, this was a yank on the collar…a sharp pull back to the reality of the state we were living in. Again, it was not the disease that was doing the damage but rather the reaction to it.

As the working week creaked itself into action, I spent many an hour on conference calls. It was disappointingly difficult to get the electricity cord to reach out to the box-balcony so, in the end, I reluctantly settled for hours sitting at the end of the bed. 2022 technology be damned! Hours spent listening in on aimless, blinkered conversations on how we were going to win the war on climate change. How banks such as ours would prove to be enlightened crusaders in the glorious battle over the World's thermostat.

I also became immersed in Wild Swans.

The book is a personal retelling of a Chinese childhood experiencing first the Cultural Revolution and then the Great Leap Forward. I could not help thinking how Mao's tunnel-visioned, famine-inducing policies could so easily be repeated as a result of today's uni-view, full-throated insistence on renewables versus fossil fuels.

I want to go down on record as having made these points. I want my sons to know that I didn't just go along to get along.

Plitvice

The standard process would see me attempting to find a holiday venue and perform a quarter-arsed job of it. Kate would then come to rescue the rapidly deteriorating situation by methodically analysing more expensive possibilities before presenting a selection of three potential answers...only one of which would be the correct one.

In a departure from this tried and tested formula, this time Kate had given me free rein to screw up.

And I very nearly did. A quick Google search had suggested a location in a national park called Plitvice. As I made a desperate third and final call, the line was ringing through and I was one iteration away from hanging up when the lovely Croation chap answered.

That one extra ring saw us land on the side of the sliding door that transported our family to an enchanted landscape that I will forever remember as my Happy Place.

Plitvice Lakes National Park.

Our accommodation was the bottom floor of what looked like a log ski chalet – one of about 20 in the camp. It was situated a one-minute walk from the restaurant and was bang next to a football pitch. An arena that would see the slapstickest family kick around of all time.

20 minutes' walk away were the waterfalls. Lakes and waterfalls. Cascades of mountain rivers, scrambling, clattering over themselves to then serenely gather in the huge glass lagoons, before again tumbling down to a lower-level, sibling rock pool.

Wooden walkways inconspicuously meandered in and out, alongside and even under the incessant rushing of diamond-clear water.

A water clock, marking the passing of time. Perpetually. A constant measure of our immediate experience in the context of an ineffably larger, eternal system. Water, as time, rushing past. Flowing from the mountains high in the range, having been coaxed from the ephemeral clouds ushered upwards by the rocky monoliths. Clouds formed by the moisture relinquished from the oceans that themselves were nourished by the rivers…sourced from the mountains.

And so on and so forth.

An everlasting, cyclical timepiece powered through the golden fusion of thermal heat. From our sun. Itself part of a cosmic cycle – a nebula born of a black hole - stretching way back to the Big Bang…and beyond.

It was awesomely, soul-warmingly beautiful. Deafeningly peaceful.

In addition, we had struck true gold. Autumn gold. The trees that horded the surrounding hills, cramming themselves in for a lignin-growing lifetime of mellifluous meditation, had just turned. Orange, orange-brown, pink, auburn, roan, rust, titian, copper, brass, bronze, terracotta, chestnut and every blend in between.

In acknowledgment to their beauty, the flawlessly smooth Plitvice pools held up sharp mirrors reflecting the overwhelming forest display. An arboreal appreciation of the annual cycle.

You can see that I lapsed into a hopeless, pseudo-philosophical trance there.

An alternative description might be that the scenery resembled an imaginary cartoonscape from a Pixar movie. The Croods. It was the magical wonderland of a colourful, happy imagination…made real.

I gushed, like the waterfalls. And then gushed some more. Also like the waterfalls.

This was to be the environment from where I would submit my resignation. Where I would cut the cord on a life and lifestyle into which I had invested 27 years of my life. A life that was, until that moment, running in parallel far away in a glass-fronted, 38-floor skyscraper in Hong Kong. An electronic buzz filling the office and acting as a less perpetual, a less sustainable passing of a finite life.

A life that, at that moment, I felt fully…deeply, profoundly at peace at leaving behind.

I serenely sent my electronic resignation missive.

And we all moved on.

Dalmation Coast

After our three magical days in Plitvice, our next venue was a very compact, domed house outside Primosten that we had found on AirBnB. A rarely-used path presented the only space between our back garden and the Dalmatian Coast. The tideless Adriatic relentlessly, hypnotically lapped at the rocks. It felt wonderfully isolated. The garden, the coast and their imaginations provided all the entertainment that the Boys required.

I had arrived a little tense. Whilst I was sublimely at ease with my decision to take a different route and leave the corporate life, there was still a lot to worry about as I awaited the official fall out from my resignation.

My difficult Hong Kong boss had recently been encouraged to move on (to retirement), but he would still be able to write the script of my departure. It was perfectly possible that he would enforce my notice period and insist that I return to Hong Kong (via three weeks' hotel quarantine). It was also likely that he would be difficult about paying out my notice period.

These were high impact questions for me and so I was keen to secure some certainty and move on to enjoying being with my family.

When we finally did manage to convene a conference call (my Hong Kong boss, my London boss and his boss) it was not a pleasant one. Hong Kong boss was again quick to draw battle lines, the bank versus me. He even, on that call, insisted that I return all devices back to the bank as soon as was humanly possible.

I was taken aback. And, it's true to say, emotional. It had been 21 years that I had poured my goodwill into that institution and, at the flick of a switch, it was an angry corporate that was seeking to intimidate me. This was in stark contrast to the employee-first, do-gooder corporate family that was so fawningly pushed by Human Resources.

To be fair, it was only one of the three bosses that behaved like that. I am sure he had his own issues to deal with...background stress that caused him to use my resignation, a(nother) tarnish on his management competence, as a vent to decompress. Some people are simply careerists with unusually nasty temperaments.

Maybe my pseudo-philosophy was germinating but I was able to get over that confrontational, poisonous exchange pretty easily. And, indeed, put it to good use as a reason to enjoy an early Croatian lager, watching the sea stream in and out of the contours of the rocks, as the Boys set afloat a palm-leaf dreadnought manned by an acorn army of eager seaman.

Who needs plastic toys.

Sweet Home

By this stage, Kate and I had become unflappable, COVID-era travelling afficionados and had all our pandemic paperwork in hand for our return to the UK. We obtained a quickfire, cheap (RACKET!) lateral flow test from a hugely entertaining and charismatic trans(sexual/vestite) doctor in advance of our flight home. To say (s)/he was blasé about the process would be a distinct understatement. (S)/he told us that all the tests were always negative, as they had nowhere to house positive cases.

Nevertheless, the next day we were to discover at the check-in desk that the negative test certificate failed on two fronts: it was only in Croatian when a UK translation was required; and it had been issued by a non-acceptable Croatian region. Who knew. Whilst this led to the wholly unnecessary stress of finding the airport lateral flow test centre and waiting for the "in 30 minutes" result, the whole performance had the feel of another confected but ultimately never journey-endangering hurdle to clamber over. RACKET!!

But, that wrinkle aside, I will always look back on our half-term trip to Croatia with overwhelming fondness. It is a wonderful, unpretentious, culture-soaked corner of the Mediterranean to which I passionately would like to return.

However, the trance-like dreamlands of Plitvice and the Dalmation Coast were soon replaced with a Halloween, northern hemisphere November and the traditional Christmas run-in.

Guy Ween Night

In a wonderfully British way, Halloween blurred into Guy Fawkes night…at least as far as the Boys could work out. For Halloween, we were invited around to a friend from my childhood's house for an afternoon bash. After a fractious preparation pulling together improvised costumes whilst working out logistics, we hiked the 30 minutes there through a hurried, biting wind that so often marks the turning of a UK autumn into winter…when the clocks go back. There were numerous familiar faces from long ago. In addition, I suffered the chronologically confusing introduction to teachers a decade younger than me who were in senior positions at my old senior school.

The event was broadly agreed to be the first meet-up of its kind since COVID and there were still some who thought it sufficient a risk to give it a swerve.

But I had fun reminiscing, Kate enjoyed chatting to a number of Mums and Dads and the Boys excelled themselves by being easy-going, cheerful and mixing happily across the age groups.

Of course, just as the evening's trick or treating began, icy splinters of rain began to dart down from the early darkness. Thankfully, R&R had quickly approached their confectionary limit and we withdrew to the warmth and familiarity of the Sunday sofa with a satisfied aplomb.

It was good to have met up and connected with more of the Shrewsbury crew and I was hopeful that this would lead to a natural expansion in our social circle.

The following weekend, we went straight from school to Manchester for a fireworks night at the local rugby club with my sister's family. It was an enjoyably chaotic, English affair. Tickets were sold out, so we snuck around to an external viewing point where the banter-keen "security guard" (/rugger bugger in high viz) ferried us discarded tins of cider and black as we froze waiting for the main event.

It turned out that my sister had mixed up rugby clubs and we had arrived at one where the fireworks were an hour later.

The display was excellent, the cousins and Boys were thrilled and we headed back home for a satisfied sleep.

But not before I had a cider and black-powered chat to my Big Sis! She had clearly been going through a similar thought process to me – questioning whether she really wanted to be beholden to a corporate existence for the rest of her working life. Whether the emotional investment, which we know is not reciprocated, can really be maintained as a rewarding pathway from middle into old age.

I wonder just how many people get the chance, take the time, to ask themselves the same question.

Of course, there are always some incredibly strong arguments to be addressed. The security of an income stream, a pension, a paid holiday allowance to set against the constant stream of expenses that form a persistent headwind – forcing one's gaze down to just the next few steps ahead.

However, my sister, I would argue, invested more emotion into her work – or, more specifically, in the people at her work – than most. And she has so much talent, creativity, sense of community betterment and passion to bring all of that together.

Her husband joined in what became something of a bonfire night, kitchen intervention. As the red wine paradoxically cleared the misty thinking of early-stage drunkenness and led us all to bright-lined certainty, she swore that she would no longer be with her company in a year's time!

This would be a conversation we would revisit numerous times before we left for Australia.

We pulled ourselves together with coffee and toast on the Sunday morning before heading off for a team walk consisting of the four youngsters (I could no longer call my 12-year-old niece a kid) my sister and me. It was a typical early winter morning, coldish, cloudy-ish, with occasional sun, a bit of wind.

It was whilst we sat down and drank our respective coffees and hot chocolates that we threw around ideas on a topic close to every parent's heart – education and how that sits within schooling systems.

I was interested in the UK's 11+ exams. Was it really something that we wanted to be doing, asking our children to equate the joy of learning with the stress of sitting down and being marked (via multiple choice questions – ie no opportunity to show workings or individuality) before they even hit puberty?

To discuss. Maybe some good reasons for and some against, but I was taken aback when my sister became quite confrontational and pointedly made the comment that I should think carefully before imposing my ethics on my children.

This came at me from such an unexpected and strange angle that I had neither thought how to field the question, nor did I field it very well. And the discussion was shelved.

Of course, I have since had a lot of time to think about it. The exchange shines a light on a remarkable, recurring phenomenon of which we should all be aware: how policies that might sneak through in inoffensive terms and presented as being a preliminary trial can, decades later, become socially entrenched, any deviation from which is deemed to be somehow extreme. Even when time has ensured that the technological, social and economic landscape has changed beyond recognition.

What was once experimental, with all sides acknowledging that future review and adaptation is crucial, can become a societal norm that, if you diverge from it, casts you in the light of reckless renegade.

My vested interest in education has seen me read *Weapons of Mass Instruction* by *John Taylor Gatto* and some time ago *Free to Learn* by *Peter Gray, The Element* by *Ken Robinson* and *The Coddling of the American Mind* by *Greg Lukianoff & Jonathan Haidt*. I think the very least we can say, with certainty, is that a once size fits all approach designed in the early 1900s and with a mind to training the vast majority to become productive factory workers is one that needs to be adapted to the modern World.

Knowing what I know now and discovering vastly erudite analyses on the questions I have been asking myself from a young age, I am genuinely quite angry that no-one directed me towards humanity's existing wealth of wisdom. Insights born of some of the greatest thinkers the World had ever seen.

And that was whilst being lavished with one of the most expensive educations money can buy. Why? Why is that?

I spent my 17th and 18th years practicing and repeating previous A-level maths exam papers because it was known that examiners recycled a limited number of questions over the years.

I rote-learnt maths solutions. For fuck's sake.

My Father

I can't tell you how much I loved my father. He was the warmest most charismatic person I have ever had the pleasure of spending time with. He gifted me his time from when I was very young, letting me hack around a golf ball behind him with a sawn off 7-iron from the age of five – we would end up racking up 100s of hours of golf together over the course of my youth.

We would go to the pub together. He was very much a man of the 70s and the pub was a foundation stone to his life. Whether it was his post-work 6 o'clock club, dominoes on a Sunday night or a Saturday afternoon Five (/Six) Nations rugby match, it was nearly always a good idea to pop to the pub.

I know in his profession he was a respected and loved anaesthetist who endeared himself to doctors, nurses and porters alike - and, of course, patients - with his easy-going, caring bedside manner.

He loved a late-night chinwag and relished his teenage children returning from their nights out with friends for a night cap and joining in – encouraging – the discussions. His sing-songy Welsh-accented "Better get a bottle of wine from the cellar" became a slogan fondly mimicked by my friends.

But tragically, he gave credence to the cliché that doctors make the worst patients. He ignored tell-tale symptoms for far too long and finally lost his battle with bowel cancer when I was 33 years old. He passed away never having seen (or knowing that he would have) grandchildren, which is something that I have to remind myself to be philosophical about.

I mention this because Mum and I took the opportunity of my being back in the UK for an elongated period to attend to his grave. I had not visited for a long, long time. It was roughly a three-hour drive away through the windiest, stop-startiest of Welsh country roads, so a six hour round trip.

It is interesting. Because I don't really *believe* in visiting his grave. He's not there. I visit him in my head, in my memories, whenever I want. And I feel much closer to him in doing that than I do standing in front of a marble headstone, ankle deep in the damp, Welsh grass behind a severe-looking church.

That mostly makes me sad. And regretful. Regretful that we buried him so far away and didn't have a proper knees up back in Shrewsbury, where we had the service.

He would have wanted a proper pub-party. But we were grief-stricken, had no instructions from him and so went with the path of least resistance. With the social norm.

I know – am certain – it was the wrong thing to have done. But done it is, now, and I am reconciled to that headstone in that graveyard presenting itself as the official memory of my beloved father.

*A word of advice to you all...*let your loved ones know how you want your mortal vehicle to be dealt with once your soul has transcended! For me it's cremation. Ideally, then being compacted into a pebble and thrown into the sea, any sea. But not that fussed if it's just the ashes scattered in the air on the M40. Stardust to stardust, ultimately.

Mum and I dutifully scrubbed off the moss, pulled away aging flowers, added new ones together with fresh water. We did the same for our nearby relations. We shed our silent tears and were both relieved to depart and be on our way home.

Despite all the above, it was somehow an important journey for Mum and me to have made. And to have made it together.

We had a pub lunch steak and headed home to Shrewsbury.

My Mum

I have already told you about my mother's amazing, sunny disposition. But she has also had the most amazing life. She was born in North-Western Germany in 1939. Her first memories are from the War, hiding a butter urn in the fields as the Nazis approached, hiding underground as bombs rained down, hunting for rabbits in the field and keeping warm around a small home fire.

From sepia, wartime Germany, to determining her own medical education, traveling as a solo woman from Germany to South Africa (she met my father on board ship where he was working as a swashbuckling, uniformed ship's doctor), upping sticks and moving to London with only a rudimentary command of the English language.

My mother has both a zest for life but also a wonderfully natural gift in story-telling. More often than not it is after a glass or two of bubbles, but we have always deeply savoured her setting off on wonderfully retold reminiscences.

The problem has been that we were always too "in the moment" to take mental - never mind written – notes or to switch on a voice-recorder. Because of this, I was determined not to let another opportunity slip by. I downloaded a voice-recorder app and sat down with Mum for 30-to-60-minute stints, starting from her first memories to today. Everything about doing that was heart-warming.

I dearly loved hearing the stories, the twinkle in my mother's eye portrayed the pride and enjoyment she felt in telling them. Rex would slip into the lounge and onto the facing sofa, normally freshly showered and in his pyjamas, to silently listen – listen to a World and life that will forever remain incomprehensible.

I like to think I had enough conscious experience of the late 70s and 80s as a child to remember a time when leaving work at 5pm meant that you would have zero interaction with that compartment of your life until 9am the next day. Only friends and family called…on the landline.

But Mum brought the 1960s and 70s to life: the reduced access to the globalised World necessitating stronger connections with those in your physical realm; the bravery of making enormous decisions that would dictate one's life and relationships (even phone calls to family would be prohibitively expensive); the relatively accepted sexism, nationalism (she is German, don't forget) and racism.

As a result, I have a treasured set of seven mini-interviews. I look forward to adding to them when I next see her in Shrewsbury or Australia.

Run in

So, we entered into a bit of a "living in Shrewsbury with my mother as the boys go to my old prep school" routine. Kate and I joined the Shrewsbury Club, which we essentially used as a gym.

All the while in the background, I endured the niggly stress of work wanting me to sign some bizarre agreement whereby I committed to never saying anything negative – or perceived to be negative - about the bank. At the same time, my Hong Kong boss was trying to short-change me with regard to payments under my notice period. This led to the angriest call I can remember having in my entire working career. The argument was about whether it should be a three months' paid notice or five. A nothing burger for the bank. Not even a rounding error. But it translated to months of living expenses in Australia.

A paradox of us living in Shrewsbury for so much longer than planned yet not being on holiday, was that it made it much harder to catch up with friends elsewhere. Had we all four been on holiday, it would have been simple to cruise around the country at non term time rates for a quick pub dinner here, kitchen supper there. However, with the Boys at school and with the accompanying birthday parties, etc, such trips were next to impossible.

However, we did enjoy a number of new experiences as we amped up our UK Christmas.

I am not one for musicals, generally. However, I was up for a local amateur dramatics performance of Elf at the local River Seven theatre.

I should have known better.

It is hard to put into words but some music-plus-singing stage combinations I just cannot endure.

Shrewsbury's production of Elf was such a combo. By the end of the first half, I was hunched in the airplane brace position, staring at the toe caps of my boots and desperately applying all the mindfulness techniques I could mentally retrieve.

By the time the audio oasis of the intermission arrived, it was beyond discussion. I had to eject. As the audience filed out into the lobby, I talked about the storyline in the past tense. Airily, I remarked that everyone would have enjoyed the show and that it was just the right length.

For a few guilt-drowning moments Rex bought the story, "yeah, Dad". It was a relief when, after a pause, he followed with, "but wait, Dad…".

It was a Chrimbo musical for kids. I couldn't go through with the selfish deception.

Mercifully, Kate (who had also suffered, if to a lesser extent) rode to the rescue and suggested I see out the second half in the pub across the street.

A better person than me would have sucked up the second instalment. But I was not that person and greedily jumped at the offer to sip a pint of real ale on my own in the Anchor…rather than discover the trilled conclusion to the story of Elf!

At the other end of the spectrum, I was happily surprised by a church sing song. Mum had secured two hugely sought-after tickets to a performance in Shrewsbury's St Chad (with a circular nave) of Ex Cathedra.

Ex Cathedra is a famous UK choir that I had previously heard of only in passing. They sing choral classics from the 12th to the 21st centuries. And they were awesome. As in, they inspired awe. Whilst their mastery of their own voices in solo and unison was obvious, I experienced for the first time a sense of parts of the brain resonating. Parallel, harmonious vibrations.

I wouldn't say a spiritual sensation rather one imbued with the collective wisdom of the ages. As if the vocal creations filling the circular nave were the products of musicians over millennia. Musicians who understood how music...song…can accord with links into the inner human.

Synapses in my cranium lit up that night in a way that I had not before experienced. That felt awesome. That thought awesome. Or some sensation in between feeling and thought.

Either way, Ex Cathedra was awesome!

Re-'Rona

Despite neither Kate nor I working, it was surprisingly easy to fill the day with what seemed necessary tasks. Of course, working out in the Shrewsbury Club or long walks along the river Seven fell unambiguously under the definition of necessary.

And with the Boys coming out of school at around 3pm, that always denoted the beginning of the end of the day – especially as November drew into December.

It was over my mother's birthday weekend at the end of November that, all of a sudden, a new wave of 'Rona hysteria burst onto our television screens. Per the Greek alphabet, it should have been called "Nu", but that would have been confusing. A new Nu variant. "Xi' was clearly a non-starter from the perspective of the people pulling the strings... and so it came to pass, that "Omicron" was conceived as the devilish new version of the bug that immediately caused hissy demands for new lockdowns.

By this stage, I was becoming unreservedly impatient with how many people were brainwashed. It felt as if someone had clicked a remote control that caused everyone robotically reach for their breath-sodden masks and auto-moronically socially-distance.

Was this going to ruin our last full family Christmas before we re-planted ourselves in Australia?

Boris

Now, I don't think I had any option at the UK 2019 General Election. Bumbling Boris or commie Corbyn. But a chunk of me was genuinely optimistic that Boris might be a free-marketeering libertarian (however you care to define that).

I can remember that optimism being boosted by his speech at Greenwich in early February 2020.

But seeing him wave through fascist policies enforced by law - imprisoning free people in their own home, preventing families from seeing each other, even from their death bed, etc – I had grown to see him as the worst, most criminal PM in the history of the United Kingdom.

I got him wrong, I was willing to concede.

But there is part of me, the bit that knows how little I know, that reminds me that some wankers like to talk about politics being "the art of the possible". Who knew what the hell was happening behind the scenes. What had caused this coordinated obliteration of our Western freedoms.

But, as Boris withstood the crazed bleating from the usual suspects, might it be that he was doing as much as he could to keep us as free as possible?

Certainly, as the UK luxuriated in relatively minor restrictions, the rest of Europe was frantically trying to out-hyperventilate themselves in an orgy of mass insanity. Italy had gone most of the way to outlawing the unvaxxed from life. Greece was beginning to *fine* the unvaxxed.

By comparison, the UK was a reckless loose cannon firing liberty cannonballs.

Yes, we had maddening mask mandates. However, by this stage anyone with a modicum of sense and backbone knew to declare to whichever audience was present that they had an "exemption". I quickly grew to quite enjoy this performance, often to the embarrassment of those accompanying me.

Interestingly, the whole Omicron hysteria was targeted at encouraging those who had already taken the death jab twice to go for the booster. In for a penny, eh? It was noticeable that they had given up on persuading, haranguing, shaming the sensible, steadfast side effect-free minority! Was this about clearing expensive stocks of fast-expiring clot shots? Could our governors be that cynical? Even as the CEO of Moderna was telling people how less effective their "vax" was for this "variant".

I desperately tried to find out what was the definition of a "new variant". I found some fluffy stabs at how many mutations equals a new variant but it all read like suspiciously inexact science.

It was also instructive to see the UK press at work in real time. I was still following as many of the balancing voices as I could and so it was frustrating to see the MSM catastrophise and extrapolate the harms of the sniffle-crom. At the same time the very South African medic who "discovered" Omicron was furiously trying to elbow her way into some airtime to re-emphasise how benign Omicron had proved to be from the outset.

The UK press was involved in a cheap deceit – one on which I had a clear line of sight. An incredibly destructive and harmful deceit. Beyond measurement.

A significant element of the fraud was the obfuscation of the direct link between COVID policies and the ruination that it has already started to cause.

On a personal level, what had been a social life firmly shifting through the gears was knocked back into a decelerating freewheel.

I had lined up a number of social events and was desperately hoping that the run-in to Christmas would provide the pub catch-ups with mates that I had so been craving. And by whose non-occurrence I was increasingly upset.

Events played out as if they were designed to taunt me. Not only would I be deprived of mates, beer and pub but the premise for that privation was to be the transparently harmless, branded Omicron variant.

Bless her, Kate was not going to allow this prolonged insanity to put the dampners on the Christmas segment of our World Detour...and a road trip to London was born!

A strong sketch was drafted and we headed down to the Big Smoke.

Chrimbo in London

We all took the three-hour car journey down to London in our stride. Even the navigation through the hellish mid-afternoon city congestion did not cause the expected traffic tension and we found our rented apartment with relative ease.

It was situated just south of Waterloo Bridge. The next day we walked miles and miles with the Boys – a full day traipsing from Waterloo to the Natural History Museum to China Town before then indulging in the Back To The Future musical.

The Lion King had been cancelled at very short notice (because one of the cast had come into contact with an Omicron-positive case – honestly). And so, we spent a ton on tickets for Back To The Future.

It was made memorable before we entered the theatre, as Kate and I had to take an on-the-spot lateral flow test in the queue, whilst the vaxxed were waved through ahead of us. Hunched over my backpack on the pavement and in-front of Rex and Raf, we scrambled to unwrap two over-packaged tests, scrape the back of our nasal cavities with the all-too-familiar swabs and drip the drips onto the plastic tray of truth. All in the name of science (/coercion).

The musical did provide a sensational performance and Raf signed off the evening by throwing some serious shapes at the back of the auditorium as the spectacular climax was delivered.

The Boys were not as impressed as we had hoped but the performance was a uniquely London experience and another one that will have been absorbed into their subconscious. So I told myself.

As part of our schedule, I had lined up a lunch with some of my favourite bank colleagues. This included my old boss who, many years prior, had rescued me from a team within the bank that caused me profound misery. He had helped set me on a path to relative success in his team that was both interesting and had fun. I had not seen him for a couple of years and so it was disappointing that these arrangements were limply let lapse as the general response to the Omicron hysteria was to stay at home and hope that the bed-wetting mess cleared itself up!

We took the overland train to our old stomping ground of Battersea and I was very grateful to meet up with my enjoyably argumentative ex-colleague from Hong Kong.

Battersea felt as if it had been preserved in aspic. The dates on the calendar had changed but little else. I felt a deep sense of gratitude for us having taken the opportunity to work abroad and also of my old life almost being behind a glass screen. A parallel reality from which I was perceptively divided. I loved looking at it and experiencing the nostalgia it prompted. But it underlined the fact that I and our family had irrevocably moved on.

I did get to meet up with some very dear old friends. On the whole, people were keen to entertain sceptical views but at the same time they had not seen each other for months and months. At one wonderfully warm kitchen supper it was the first time two good friends had seen each other for 18 months despite living a mile apart.

My treat night, in an old favourite drinking pub, crumbled into a non-event. Whilst everyone seemed to be symptom-free, the insistence that they take lateral flow tests saw them test Omicron-positive and therefore pub-negative.

Another, bon homie, back-slapping pub night frustratingly thwarted!

But we all benefitted a huge amount from our London trip. From Kew Gardens to the Science Museum to China Town, a solid sprinkling of reconnections with beloved friends. And we even managed to finish off on the final Saturday morning with a sneaky visit to the anti-mandate protests outside the Houses of Parliament. It was enrapturing people-watching. Both Kate and I could have spent hours strolling amongst the wildly diverse ranks of the equally sceptical…and beyond!

But the Boys were tiring after some huge London days and were ready for a solid narrating from Stephen Fry's Troy audiobook on the three-hour journey home to Shropshire.

The rest of the Xmas run-in was uneventful. Disappointingly quiet. There was way too much discussion about who should take lateral flow tests and when. After nearly two years of sunk-cost sacrifices, no-one wanted to thoughtlessly butcher their granny with a runny nose – especially not at Christmas time.

So, nights out were cancelled until Christmas Eve when the whirlwind that is my sister and her family blew into Shrewsbury.

Hey – at least there was New Year. As a plethora of other "blow out with mates" events were reluctantly surrendered, this beacon shone on the horizon as my opportunity to let rip with friends from way back.

But only until the day after Boxing Day.

It was a convoluted sequence of associations, non-symptomatic but lateral flow positive events that led to my New Year reunion also being canned.

New Year Cheer and Beer

I can be somewhat of a fatalist. An "oh well, that was that" kinda guy and I would probably have let plans lapse.

But bless her. Kate would not let it go. We hurriedly scanned random corners of England for a night's accommodation, exchanged messages and calls and cobbled together a revised New Year plan.

After a night in a cosy pub in Wilton, we visited Stonehenge for a bit of compare and contrast with the Greco-Roman ruins in Spain.

However, it being New Year's Eve, the urge to pitch camp and start boozie celebrations took over and we departed after a fleeting visit.

We had a cracking night. A long, lazy kitchen supper with a much-loved friend from school but with whom I had become much closer during our Battersea bachelor days. He also had two sons and so there was a natural source of entertainment for the Boys.

It had been a long, long time since I had stayed up to 3am setting the World to rights but this was magnificent and well worth the price that was inevitably paid as we woke up to a New Year's Day with some dusty driving to be done!

Post New Year, we had fancied a UK road trip. The concept of a "road trip" always sound better than the reality but I had been trying to wrench commitments from various friends who were more spread out around the country than when I had departed seven years ago.

And it did feel as if I had to be insistent.

Of course, this could purely have been the manifestation of fading friendships or old mates not being that fussed to see me. However, by this stage I had gathered a firm sense that everyone was just that bit happier to be left alone…reluctant to make an effort to change their routine. To leave their home.

But butt in, we did! And it was truly a terrific way to kick off the New Year. That insistence of not taking no for an answer paid off for everyone. We ended up driving many a mile, all the way down to North

Devon before rebasing ourselves in Shrewsbury for our last few days before, I suppose…emigrating.

Strange how that word meant so very much – a monumental wholesale change to one's life – yet for us it felt like the eagerly awaited natural progression.

I was pleased. There was a number of friends that I had not managed to meet up with, or only for a fraction of the time that I would have liked. However, simply touching base, reconnecting eye contact, strongly felt to me as if it would help sustain those friendships far more robustly into the future.

Until the next time!

Male Mates

As a male, I think there is a level of friendship attained with those whom you grew up over the ages 12 to 18 that cannot be matched. From boy to young man. From 100% parent-dependent to university allowance-dependent. From hairless to hairy – smooth to stubbly. Ambivalent to randy. Recipient of ideas to generator. Sober to drunk. Your parents' child to your own man.

The experiences that are welded into our memories on that journey shape who we are. As a bloke, to experience that step-change in so short a period of time is a defining process in who we become. The interactions, support, ribbing, humour, comradery, fights we accumulate from our friends over that metamorphosis feed into a huge proportion of our future thoughts and actions.

The elements we like or admire in our friends become woven into our adult selves. Whether consciously or subconsciously, a fragment of us is a piece assimilated from our mates.

I still catch myself in certain situations adopting mannerisms picked-up from those with whom I grew up.

Imitation is the sincerest form of flattery.

And I was life-changingly lucky to have some of the best people you are ever likely to meet in my year at school. I might not convince anyone but, despite being pupils at an eye-wateringly expensive public school, I found myself in a year with the most down-to-earth, good-hearted crew I could have hoped for.

Whilst I am unarguably detached from the group, having taken to leaving the UK, I am supremely comfortable that I will be able to pick up where we left off, most likely over a pint, whenever we next find a moment to catch up.

Genuine, life-long friends who know me well enough to allow me to say what I think.

Beer & Curry

If you were to ask me to describe my perfect night out, it would be four to six of my closest mates in a pub…for HOURS…probably watching Wales beat England at rugby followed by a slapstick session in a curry house. Just talking a lot of nonsense for hour after hour.

As my birthday approached, on the Friday of the last weekend before we were due to fly out of the UK, I did my utmost to get as close to that Utopia as was feasible two weeks into a dark, dank January. My birthday's situation in deepest winter has always seen it face the challenge of prizing folk from their centrally-heated living rooms just weeks after the calendar's biggest double blow-out of the year.

So, I was already over-excited at having secured two hours in a pub followed by a booking at the next-door Indian eatery with two other couples. If you added together the ages of the two husbands at the time we first became friends, you would reach the ripe total of 11. We went back a long way.

I was in fine cheer as I swung through the pub doors at 6pm and eagerly ran my eyes across the generous selection of ales on offer at the bar.

As I drew out this thoroughly enjoyable process, an unidentified voice angled in from behind me, "mate, I'll get these". I swung around and my brain pressed pause. Neurons misfired and synapses had to re-align themselves in order to assess the situational non sequitur. The kind offer had come from one of my very best friends – indeed, my best man. Why was he here? He happened to be visiting his parents? But they had left Shrewsbury some years ago?

One by one, my mental pathways reorganised themselves in time to take in a number of familiar faces from a table in the corner.

Kate had organised a surprise visit from three of my oldest mates. They had come up from Godalming for a single night out on the beers. Furthermore, she had arranged that I stay the night in a hotel opposite another town pub, this one famed for its late-night lock-ins.

My inability to put together a coherent sentence conveyed that I had lost the power of speech.

But a frothing local ale or two soon soothed the shock and we all cheerily launched into a good old knees-up.

By the time we had clattered and mis-ordered our way through a delicious array of curried cuisine, it was standard last orders. But the late-night pub held to its reputation and delivered. To my pub-starved eyes it was an after-hours wonderland of flowing ale, laughter and bon homie.

Kate had even thought to leave a night cap bottle of wine in my room, which was duly shared over a garbled conversation about Brexit.

It was a rip-roaring night and a magnificent celebration with which to bid my friends and the shores of Blighty a boozy farewell.

It was a relief to spend the following night, my actual birthday, with just my mother and sister in a pub close to home for a steak dinner. No need for anything more extravagant than that!

Adie-UK

We all knew it was coming. We all had emotions that needed processing. And we all knew it was on the minds of each of us.

But, of course, we weren't able to communicate these feelings effectively.

And so, the last few days before our departure were spent awkwardly focusing on the logistics of packing, paying bills and cleaning the granny flat that had been our home for just under five months.

Our leaving had been a long time coming...and it meant such a deep, deep wrench. The Boys had grown accustomed to their habitual Omi cuddles on the sofa (and, even more so, vice versa). The depth of bonds that had been created over the five months of us living with Mum meant that we had entered new territory in terms of how to navigate our goodbyes.

Awkward, rushed, tearful...deeply sad. Impatient for it to be over so that each of us could begin processing.

I told the Boys that how much you miss people is a function of how much you love them – and how lucky we were to have that richness of love in our family.

Suddenly, it did very much feel as if we were emigrating to the other side of the World.

Dubai Lay-by

Happily, we had arranged to spend 10 days in Dubai with our dearest friends from Hong Kong – our "Oogah!" Friends. They had departed the Special Administrative Region at the same time as us but with the contrasting challenge of setting up their new lives in Dubai.

This intermission provided both something to look forward to in the very immediate future as well as a welcome decoy for our sense of loss.

They also have a son in between the ages of Rex and Raf. And a fawned-over dog.

Arriving was quite the event. Due to "vaccine" restrictions on airlines, we had to fly to Abu Dhabi and then take a one-hour taxi to our friends' house. But before being released from the airport we had to take a(nother) PCR test in a cordoned-off section of the airport. There were various stations attended by what appeared to be students hidden underneath ill-fitting, white bio-suits.

Having landed just before midnight, time was drifting into the early hours as we handed over our passports to be digitally attached to the DNA samples inexpertly excavated from deeper-than-necessary in our nasal cavities.

The paid, part-time plums in their over-sized hazmat suits seemed to scrape and shuffle around like mummies, holding their bio-hazard snot capsules as if they contained Ebola.

If only our friends in Wuhan had been so diligent.

Anyway, with our personal genetic code presumably stored in an airport fridge alongside our work-experience friends' Red Bull, we were free to be released into the UAE. An hour later we tip-toed into our hosts' spatial Dubai home at about 2am.

The next couple of days were a blur of drinking, meat and fantastic chat. It's lucky that we all had the luxury of time, as we had so much to catch up on, from the personal to the global, that it took two days for us all to calm down. It was only after that weekend that we thought about exploring our surroundings.

Dub-Highway

There are some plus sides to Dubai. Two would be that it has a zero rate of income tax and that it is brilliantly situated for travel to many parts of the World (Europe, India, SE Asia).

But there are also numerous downsides. Whilst weather in January is lovely, the searing heat in summer is less hospitable than in Hong Kong. Everything is a drive away – normally via an air-cooking concrete highway of up to six lanes. As a result of the summer heat, nearly everything needs to be inside.

But what blew me away is how expensive it is to go out. To go out-out. If you wanted to have a big night with dinner, drinks and dancing think over US$ 500 per head.

I just cannot enjoy myself that much. Call me a grinch. But I can't. And I probably didn't!

There are alternatives. I found a small curry and kebab café close to where we were staying that was below US$ 10 for dishes I found perfectly delicious. But such venues are purely functional eating places that are not allowed to serve that fundamental Western necessity, alcohol.

The opportunity to differentiate markets (that is, to target the richer, booze-centric expat community) via alcohol has been truly embraced in Dubai. To the point where the clientele that you find in the establishments serving wine and spirits are beyond counting the cost of a night out.

But we did have an utterly amazing time. At the Atlantis water park, the Boys consummately displayed their differing temperaments. Rex's face of utter horror as we whooshed down one of the family slides in what was a re-enforced paddling pool saw him tap out of any more rides for the day. Instead, he chose to relax in what was a water-doused playground. In contrast, I was frogmarched by Raf to the top of the Leap of Faith "experience". The queue for the jump off a 14m vertical wall (you have to "leap" without being able to see the slide beneath that will decelerate you from terminal velocity) was abuzz with nervous adults, hopping from foot to foot and looking over their shoulders curiously at the ice-cool seven-year-old stood next to me.

I have never been the best with heights. Frankly, I get vertigo. Although I have found, like when you stare at the ground out of an airplane window, that the stomach-clenching apprehension disappears the more unnatural the height threat.

I even managed a sky-dive in Queensland when I was 29. I was nervous but not vertiginous.

However, the 14-metre-high view of the rest of the water park was immediate enough to create sufficient vertigo for me to want to get this over and done with.

Raf couldn't wait and had to be restrained by the attendant when it seemed as if he would strut straight over the edge.

He was worryingly fearless. And he loved it. We had to listen to his retelling of just how unscary it was for the rest of the day.

We could not visit Dubai without a trip to the desert. We took a tour into the surrounding sand dunes which delivered a phenomenal experience. We were lucky to have a wonderfully informative Uzbeki driver. Amongst the many anecdotes, he recounted how since 2005 the camel racers have been using robot jockeys. Before that, immigrant children had been pressed into service as the riders but had been so badly mistreated that they would often fall off and be killed or maimed.

Once in the desert, we saw some stunningly elegant Arabian oryx and gazelles, fed the fish at a watering hold and enjoyed an apple tea as we watched a falconry display. All the time, the sand-cushioned silence provided a magical backdrop to the descent of the hazy rose sun. A wonderfully serene environment, even while being bobbed around by the arrhythmic lollop of the camel on which we rode to dinner.

The six-courser was a little unnecessary (/utterly profligate). I was beginning to develop a spending-numbness as a coping strategy and this certainly felt like a once-in-a-lifetime experience.

I am the type of person who finds making large payments for indulgences teeth-grindingly difficult at the best of times. But I had just ticked off my last official day as an employee of my bank of 22 years. I was unemployed for the first time since leaving university and with no clear grasp of how we would secure an income stream once in Australia. Supress those thoughts/worries/concerns as I did, they lurked and wriggled in my subconscious.

Maybe, I could find some inspiration at Kidzania. Kidzania was a children's entertainment centre in The Dubai Mall – a 7,000 square metre mock-up world with shops and activities arranged over two levels. Essentially, a replica town centre but inside an air-conditioned shopping complex. The concept was that children could select and attain skills that they wanted to learn in the various shops. On achieving that skill, they would be rewarded by earning KidZania tokens which could be spent on themselves. On real life crisps and chocolates.

If you were to spin the concept positively you would align with the website blurb, that KidZania provided the opportunity for children to "learn about jobs, money and the real World while developing life skills that simply cannot be taught in the classroom."

Hurrrumph! If you were to view it through my current line of thinking, you would be alarmed at the stark mapping with how most of us have been brainwashed to approach life!

We pay (a lot) to march our children into a closed, manufactured environment where they are instructed that the only way to obtain the unhealthy treats they have been programmed to lust for, is to clock up qualifications that they would otherwise have no interest in so that they can accumulate the fake money with which to purchase those processed nasties.

For Kidzania read The Corporate World…eeeek!

And the three boys loved it. The dopamine hit triggered through connecting action with a mouthful of chocolate energised those Pavlovian synapses in minutes. Ker-lick! There you have it.

Seeing Rex and Raf compare their mass-produced, confectionary booty with their Russian pal was a high-resolution snapshot pinpointing the mechanism by which we adults had been captured in a World of fiat tokens.

The Boys were in a fake town in a massive, atmospherically-controlled mall all 100% predicated on consumerism. In their minds, it was easy to imagine it was all real. Especially as they so wanted it to be real.

Whereas, they should have been picking splinters out of their thumbs from clambering that one branch too high in the back garden gum tree. Because that is real.

I was hoping I had left my corporate-controlled complex and that I would find my real climbing tree in Australia.

Shakra

Another stand-out (and expensive) experience from Dubai was Kate and me, on the recommendation of our hosts, seeing Dr David of a nearby Wellness Centre in order to have our shakras read.

I had always been intrigued by ancient insights such as shakras but had never explored them further than asking curious questions. Our host had his shakras read a few months prior and raved about the experience.

I did not ask him for too much of a preview as I was up for a new, untrailed experience.

Kate went in ahead of me, whilst I relaxed with a coffee and a book in the next-door cafe during her 90-minute session.

As her time was close to being up, I approached the centre's very friendly receptionist but found it difficult to concentrate on the questions being asked as the repeated clanging of what sounded like a table bell was followed by an unbridled, primeval female roar - from what I intuited to be my wife.

Crikey.

When Kate did finally emerge and floated down the stairs to where I was wearing a sheepish, inquiring smile I noticed that her eyes were glazed and recognised that there was zero point in asking her anything right at that moment.

I was keen to get started!

I won't go into too much detail but my meeting with Dr David started off as a light counselling session. He asked questions about traumas, what I felt guilty or ashamed about.

After the trauma of losing my father, I really struggled to come up with something seminal and I think I blathered something about my last cricket season at school and how the master in charge's attitude towards me affected the rest of my "career".

However, thereafter, it was an extraordinary experience. Through a mixture of breathing and mental exercises, he set my arms tingling. I found that I couldn't control my fists as they involuntarily clenched.

I had told Dr David that I had been thinking about spirituality, hallucinogens and whether these provided a pathway to glimpsing our sixth sense, a supra dimension above what we experience in the day to day.

And I think (for some reason, I did not ask) that is where he tried to take me with the meditative exercises. Maybe it was my mind playing tricks but, in my head, he came very close. I saw many visions pass in front of my eyelids - enjoyably vivid, these did not feel as if they came from my own conscience. And there was a moment where my mind was at the mouth of a whirlpool. A non-threatening vortex which I sensed I had to go through in order to find the next level of answers.

But that is where my experienced stopped short.

Yeeeees, I also did some of the feral roaring with the bell-ringing. And that felt good. I felt like an A student when he told me that all my shakras were open. But for some reason, I knew I would get an A on that front.

Dr David drained my wallet but delivered an experience for which I will always be grateful. And one that still leaves me wanting more!

Goodbye Dubai

Dubai had been a blow-out in every respect. We feared it would prove to be our last holiday outside of Australia for some time, as border restrictions were still being punted around as the bedraggled political football that the issue had become.

We had loved…adored…our time with our dearly cherished Russian friends. But we had taken up their space for long enough, had seen enough of Dubai and were overdue making the final leg of our World Detour.

Of course, we could not depart without the ritual PCR mayhem. First, immediately after our Dr David sessions, Kate and I endured another schnozz-scraping swab with an at-home test. Having wrongly settled into complacency with regard to being in control of the paperwork required for this stretch of our journey, we then read enough (intentional?) ambiguity into the guidelines to believe that we needed the Boys to also have negative PCR tests.

The panic button was promptly thumped, emergency testing initiated (at colossal expense) and the clock set ticking to when we could expect their results. The tests were taken at 3pm. Our flight was at midnight.

To further spice-up the excitement, our hosts' Indian home-help, with whom we had many conversations, tested PCR positive. Would we?!

As we hurtled back to Abu Dhabi airport, Kate and I each intermittently refreshed our emails to check for Boys' results. It was great relief that the document-checker at the re-purposed toll booth on the motorway only asked for the adults' test results, but we were still glancing nervously at our phones as we queued up at the check-in in the departure terminal.

As luck would have it, we had a trainee checker-inner who soon needed help with our folder of documentation (PCR tests, my Australian visa, the exemption documentation amongst others). 50 minutes into the process (still no sign of the Boys' test results...but they hadn't asked for them...) and I was getting worried.

Then, all of a sudden, a tap in the keyboard, boarding passes printed off and we are directed to the security gates.

I don't know what caused the process to take so long. The delay fired flashbacks to our original departure from Hong Kong when the novelty of the unknowns caused heart-flutter stress. By this last stage, we had remained relatively calm. Que sera sera.

But through, we were. There was just enough time for me to greedily glug down two lukewarm Heinekens before being relieved at the gate of the four US $5 water bottles I had purchased for the kids. A gentle reminder that we could not hope to escape dumb-arsed rules when we arrived Down Under.

Finally, we were on the ultimate leg to our final destination. Australia.

PART IV - POST TRANSITION

Australia

"One does not accumulate but eliminate. It is not daily increase but daily decrease. The height of cultivation always runs to simplicity."

Bruce Lee

Pre-post-Err-US!

Over Easter 2020 I had quarantined for two weeks in a Brisbane hotel and enjoyed the experience.

However, as we landed in Sydney, closing in on midnight, I had no idea what the next two weeks would look like. What I knew for sure was that this was going to be an altogether different episode. Two young boys fizzing with energy, a wife who prizes her own space and two sun-starved weeks inside stretching ahead of us.

It goes without saying that, at this stage, the concept of quarantine was wildly detached from any "science". The Queensland population was allegedly 95% vaccinated (although it was now widely accepted that this had little to no impact of transmission), Omicron was raging left, right and centre and our family had already had the bug. And been peppered with PCR tests.

But for 14 days, the Australian Government had decreed that we should be confined within the walls of an apartment in an as-yet unspecified hotel. To my mind, the nature of the apartment was going to be pivotal to how the mental health of Team McWilliams would be impacted by this bizarre procedure. I had played out a plethora of scenarios in advance and, as the light of Sydney gently amplified through the plane window, my sense of anticipation grew as I darted around my mental filing cabinet for a final flick through.

The immigration queue was tortuous, late-night chaos and we had found ourselves at the back of it. It was only after we had picked up our weary-looking baggage that our vax status caused us to be segregated for separate processing.

It took a while. Some poor chap joined us protesting that he had had the "vaccine" before having it explained to him that it was the wrong one. He had an entirely unexpected 14-day delay coming his way.

Eventually, we found ourselves on a shuttle bus to our detention centre. The journey was only notable for the background radio laconically delivering the news that the NRL (rugby league competition) was being decimated by asymptomatic players testing positive for the 'Rona.

Maybe this was a message from the divine - the facts will ultimately out?

We arrived at our hotel in a good-looking suburb of Sydney. We scribbled and signed through yet more painfully purposeless paperwork before being escorted by misassigned policemen to our quarters.

I was utterly delighted. The apartment blew through the ceiling of what I had allowed myself to hope for. We had a twin room, a double room, two bathrooms, a large kitchen living area…AND A BALCONY!!!

A balcony. A bloody balcony. This had been the one facility for which I would have forsaken all others. A breeze, some fresh air, the sense of being outside. We had it. This was going to be so much more do-able as a result.

It even over-looked the suburb's sports oval. Was I going to be able to watch live sport whilst in quarantine?

It was late. We were tired but content. Holidaymakers having arrived at their exciting new accommodation. We slid into the hotel beds and slipped to sleep.

Quaran-Team!!

Another question, the possible answers to which had been looping through my mind for months, was how to keep up doing exercise. There on the coffee table were numerous pamphlets offering a range of facilities…including a treadmill. Joy of joys! I jumped at the chance to hire one.

It arrived in a flash and we eagerly wheeled it out to the balcony. Fresh air and exercise. This was starting to blossom from do-able to enjoyable.

The balcony caught the sun from early in the morning until about 11am. My Australian quarantine would require me to remain sun-safe!

My marching missions to nowhere on the treadmill turned into something of an obsession, as I regularly revised upwards my aggregate target for our two-week stay. I ended up aiming for 250 km (I was kicking myself about how much higher this could have been had I realised my potential daily average from the outset) but reached 273km. Even on what I had sensibly reserved as my "rest day" I couldn't resist a cheeky 10km-er.

With arguably antisocial addiction, I revelled in the hailstorm of podcasts that showered down on my conveyor belt of contemplation. I noted them all down. 42 podcasts over the fortnight.

It must have presented a worrying daily sight for the boys, seeing their increasingly ungroomed father intermittently swearing/sniggering/gasping disbelievingly to himself while trudging km after km in the direction of the patio doors.

Whilst, in fact, going precisely nowhere. Hmmmm…is there a message that can be read across from that scenario?

The other key factor that had absorbed months of mental scenario-planning was that of food. And we had lots of it. Plonked outside the door. Once a day.

Three meals in plastic containers with one plastic bottle of water for each of us…for each of the three meals. Plus the plastic orange juices to accompany breakfast. Our fridge and cupboards started to overflow with plastic before our requests for NO MORE water or juice finally registered.

The food was OK. Some of it, genuinely tasty. But what made the sustenance segment of our stay sustainable was our ability to order fresh fruit, veggies and nibbles from the supermarket.

Kate and I had both vowed to go alcohol-free for the 14 days as well as takeaway-free for as long as possible. However, we had never been able to wean Rex & Raf of their inter-meal snacks and so being able to cork their whining apertures with the ripe apple was crucial.

Over the first couple of days, we had naturally experienced a solid bout of jet lag. This saw the Lads sleep in until 3pm on the first day but our inability to get them outside (and, I am sure, other aspects of our predicament) meant that their shift to Sydney time took longer than usual. Often, they would still be up at midnight, sing-whinging that they were not tired. Ingeniously, I had some "nutritional gummies" (adult, over-priced Haribo substitutes) which we managed to pass off as sleeping pills. A ruse which worked to bridge them through the first few nights.

Kate and I were strict on TV-time, but we did allow the Boys a solid dose of Winter Olympics in the afternoon and a movie in the evenings. It was an ugly bribe, but I enticed them to tread the mill for 20 minutes a time with the lure of episodes of Fawlty Towers on the iPad. I was unreservedly delighted to hear them belly-laugh at what has always been one of my all-time favourites. They found Manuel particularly hilarious.

Yes, there are plenty of moments that starkly clash with our current PC environment - I suspect that Basil and company are unlikely to be much longer for this World.

Kate spent an inordinate amount of time surgically pecking at a genuinely feisty jigsaw that my sister had been kind enough to have delivered to our confinement cell. An infuriatingly addictive, back-to-front 1,000-piece puzzle that at its zenith saw all four of us pore over the last 100 pieces at 12.30am.

When she wasn't snoozing, stealing treadmill time from me or puzzling, Kate was dutifully heaving her way through War and Peace. This was a challenge that she had set herself with the expectation of enjoying it but it's fair to say a lighter, more bubble-gum book might have been more enjoyable.

I read *David Deutsch*'s *The Beginning of Infinity*, *Robert F Kennedy Junior*'s *The Real Anthony Fauci* (shocking, just shocking) and my own sugary confection, *The Sins of the Father* by *Jeffrey Archer.*

Rex tunnelled his auburn mullet through a series of "Pegasus" books and demonstrated an astonishing staying power, reading for hours... and hours. At least until his bored younger brother would come in with various baiting prods that would swiftly escalate into emotional eruptions.

Poor Raf didn't have the attention span to indulge in obsessive distractions and literally bounced off the walls. With a mixture of clothes, pillows, beds and bedding, he created his own masonry-jolting Jumping Olympics in the Boys' room.

We made our own pizzas and took the opportunity to teach Rex how to bake.

After a few of these days, time seemed to be less and less of an enemy. Settling into a routine caused the 24-hour cycles to tick over. It was a becalming experience.

I tried to pin down why I was finding this enforced (if admittedly, luxury) incarceration so soothing.

Was it because we had so few options? Of what to do, to eat, where to go? I found the alleviation of decision-making mollifying.

And it occurred to me just how many decisions we are making in a normal working Western day. A dizzying array of choices from coffees to lunch venues, to what to read on social media, to what to watch on Netflix, etc. Have human beings been cognitively wired to navigate a constant onrush of mini options? A never-ending series of rocky rapids, constantly commanding your concentration on what is directly in front of you from second to second. No time to look up and contemplate the bigger picture…where the waterway is eventually heading.

All I can say is that I thoroughly enjoyed our time as Team Quarantine. It was with a slightly nostalgic look over our collective family shoulder that we found ourselves on our last night breaking our alcohol and takeaway ban with a crossed-legged balcony picnic. I was proud and relieved. As with so many of the aspects surrounding traveling during COVID derangement, it was the not knowing, the doubt, the imagined scenarios that caused more mental strain than the actualised process.

All that time spent thinking about how our young men would cope with being locked in with their parents for half a month…and I enjoyed it. Other than the kick-in-the-teeth A$5,000 cost, I would have chosen for us to have done this over not. It was a unique bonding experience even after six months already spent experiencing bonds.

I also mused how easy it was to kill time nowadays without getting bored. I had been confined to an apartment for 14 days with my family and not once had I been bored.

Which is it?

1) We now have amazing access to more knowledge than we will ever be able to digest and so we can learn from wherever we are, whenever we wish; or
2) Tech is cluttering up our days so much that we no longer have time to be healthily bored and contemplative.

Hmmmm!!

Free in Sydney

But we were very happy to be leaving what had been a holding bay for getting on with being in Australia.

And before launching on that final internal leg of the journey to Brisbane, we were lucky enough to revel in a couple of nights living it up with some deeply loved friends from Hong Kong. They have four children, three boys and a girl. Two of the boys were terrific, bessie mates with ours in Hong Kong. The family had headed back to Sydney in November 2019 and so had bedded in before the 'Rona and its accompanying insane policies has descended. They were a hyper-active, hyper-intelligent, hyper-hyper family and always a scream.

They lived close enough to Sydney's Eastern Suburbs beach for it to be within the allowable distance accorded by the NSW Corona restrictions. This had been crucial for their surf-crazed family and they had managed to navigate a healthy, outdoors course through COVID. On the whole, they had had a good one.

Making that connection in Aus for us as adults as well as for Rex and Raf, was an enormously important Coming Home moment. Familiar faces from pivotal times in our lives and with experiences that, when shared, still make us involuntarily splutter our drinks all over ourselves.

We luxuriated in each other's company for two days. And then it was time to head home.

Home

The journey from Sydney to the Sunshine Coast was so smooth that our arrival felt abrupt. Two years after having made the decision to move, months and months of visualising, doubting...we were there. At our new full-time home.

We had bought the house in 2018. We had reasoned that, under any realistic circumstance, we would always need a base in Australia. I had first been introduced to the Sunshine Coast Hinterland in 2014. As part of a circuitous route to Hong Kong, we visited the region for the wedding of Kate's cousin. The countryside teemed with nature. I was blown away by the views: from the top of the range the landscape charted a lush-green 30 km rolling descent into the Coral Sea. A glorious combination of mountains, sun and sea. Green, gold and blue.

If you squinted, there was a resemblance to Wales-with-sunshine! Hedgerows, hills and cow-filled fields.

Our house was perched close to the top of the embankment. Inconspicuously, contentedly soaking up the imperious views whilst happily allowing the more pronounced dwellings at the top of the range to act as a decoy for attention.

The previous retiree inhabitants had built the property 14 years earlier with great sympathy for the steep slope. They had also clearly been extremely avid, if scattergun, gardeners. The hillside boasted a Gardener's World inventory of flowers, bushes, shrubs, trees, creepers, indigenous and non-indigenous vegetation.

As we were to learn over the coming months, simplifying our home's flora and then staying on top of it would become a larger part of our lives than we had previously experienced…by an order of magnitude!

But that was a large part of the point. To be in and around nature.

I now wake up with the first inklings of dawn and can lift my head ever so slightly from my pillow to be presented with a landscape view of a magenta, Coral Sea sunrise miles out over ocean.

That's the first thing I see beyond the slender right shoulder of my sleeping spouse…whilst contentedly couched in a chorus of kookaburras and cows...punctuated with the occasional caw of a crow.

At first, I was apprehensive about the legions of creepy crawlies. I am not good with spiders and have very rarely encountered a snake in the wild.

Fascinatingly, it has only taken six months for me to be pretty much fine with the constantly twitching, rustling, clicking trees, bushes and shrubbery.

It is striking how sanitised our urban lives sit in comparison to what humans have hitherto always been used to. I know that's a cliché and am trying to make the point differently.

But it's pretty goddam normal to have a field mouse run across your path on the deck, or to have to remove a brown tree snake from the garage.

That would have sounded like wild-eyed Bear Grills survivalism to me just 12 months ago.

Is one of the reasons we are seeing so much division at the moment down to people becoming increasingly hemmed into the straight edges and bright lines of their urban dwelling. No more, the ramshackle barn or improvised gate.

That's not to say that I have become friendly with spiders. Far from it (the creepy fuckers). But I no longer yelp and flinch!

Too Easy

Most regions have their own endearing colloquial vernacular. But the Sunny Coast Queenslander takes it to a new level of laid back. Instead of a "You're welcome" or "No worries" response to when you say thank you, the local response is "Too easy".

I love that. It reflects a sense of kind, nothing-is-too-much-trouble hospitality. The Sunny Coast Queenslanders are genuinely the most friendly and easy-to-talk-to folk I have come across.

They also encourage a more general acceptance and accommodation of people. All sorts. Rich, poor, sensible, larrikin, enviro, realist…vaxxed, unvaxxed.

People may not agree to, or like, the stance you take but they accept it. And you.

On the whole…

Dine-in Denied

We had enjoyed our Queensland Easter road trip that had taken us up to Bundaberg (famous for its sugar and consequently rum) and then inland to Sapphire, Emerald and Rubyvale. As their name suggests, these were old mining towns going back over 100 years. We had made the trip as part of our Easter holidays with the hope that the idea of prospecting for precious stones (fossicking) would spark excitement in the Boys.

It was a hugely enjoyable trip and a peak into a World we hadn't seen before. There were clearly many families and individuals who had opted for a different life. Maybe out of a passion for discovering jewels… maybe borne of a desire not to go to jail! But it was an incredibly colourful community, each with their allotted claim over an area on which they would cobble together a dwelling from rusted caravans, lean-to tarpaulins and even bricks and mortar.

Kate and I were not allowed down the mine without a "vaccine" passport, but we could join the Boys for open-air panning the buckets of earth ("wash") – sifting through rubble for the illusive life-changing royal blue AA sapphire to be sold for a fortune.

And you do find some! No, not the high-end jewel-worthy ones but tiny, opaque sapphire splinters. Worth maybe 30 bucks but still a stand-out stone in a pile of rubble. There is something about the serendipity – certainly, you can see how it becomes addictive. Compulsive. A stone-aged one-armed bandit?

In the Outback with the rock wallabies, fossicking alongside the old-time dreamers in a dusty, post-boom town, this was a precious road trip experience to add to those accumulated over the last 12 months.

The distances and time I drove in that week went beyond what I had totalled over seven years in Hong Kong.

Anyway, we were clocking up kms on our way to Kate's family farm when we pulled over for lunch in a small, isolated town called Injune.

There was only one road-side café to choose from and we duly ordered our beef and chicken burgers only to have our "vaccine" passports demanded.

Over the previous two months this had not happened to us once on the Sunshine Coast.

We were in the clear to order a takeaway (whilst standing in the café) but we could not eat it on the deck outside the door. We had to take the Boys and our lunches five metres along the deck, outside the neighbouring Tourist Information Office, to eat there.

This was a stark reminder of how a captured audience had been fed a consistent line, repeated long enough for it to inculcate unthinking behaviour. The killer point here was that an announcement had already been made that the "vaccine" requirement would be repealed on the Friday. This was the preceding Wednesday.

It had become abundantly clear over our travels that it was almost impossible to predict the level of uptake and implementation of the COVID restrictions in different communities or sub-communities. A striking illustration of how emergent behaviours can mushroom to become the dominant norm as a product of random, organic group-evolution.

I counted myself lucky to be able to live in an environment where different views were tolerated. Maybe even applauded.

School ("Super Cruel Hours Of Our Lives")

Kate's five months in our home during the early days of COVID had prepared Rex and Raf for our long-term return. They settled in straight away. When I consider my childhood trauma of moving schools and starting afresh as the newbie, the Boys were exceptional. They were greeted with an almost celebrity welcome on their reappearance at the local state school.

At the same time, we enrolled them into the local soccer team, into which they also slotted effortlessly.

That Sunshine Coast welcome was repeated and amplified over the following weeks. For some intangible reason, folk were simply easy to talk to. My previous reference point of relocating ourselves was Hong Kong. There, the initial stages of making friends felt more like a Powerpoint presentation of who you are and why you are a family unit with whom it's worth investing time. It took a long time to feel relaxed enough in the presence of new friends to truly lay out who you are.

On the Sunny Coast you don't have to overthink it. Just say it how you see it. And that I love.

Naturally, our friend group is driven by the parents of the school pupils. And these are parents who put a huge amount into the school.

My previous experience of schools, throughout my childhood and to date with the Boys, was that you pay fees to experts who you entrust to create an educational environment with which you are happy.

For the first time, I was being exposed to an educational environment where the value delivered by the school is materially enhanced by the input and involvement of the parents.

This, I also loved.

It creates a joint (if not always aligned) purpose amongst the parents. It reaches across any parent-teacher divide, providing the educators with a familiarity of their pupils in a family context which is otherwise lost.

And it generates a continuous bond for the children: from the kitchen table to their schooling day to pick-up time all the way through back to dinner time and a goodnight read. When they see their parents chatting day-to-day with the principal, their form teacher, their friends' parents, the Boys can see that they and their family form an important piece of a greater schooling community.

That's not to say I am won over by the school system in Australia.

I don't know what quantum of it is driven by the transition from a private to a public, state school but coming to the Sunshine Coast it is striking how prevalent home-schooling is. Indeed, how many of the parents had been home-schooled.

Home-schooling is not something I ever came across as I grew up and only really came to my attention when the Hong Kong schools were first forced to shut down due to COVID.

In a ridiculous, hapless attempt to justify a continuation of their extortionate school fees, the private schools in Hong Kong implemented a painfully inadequate on-line learning regime.

When you are presenting a woefully deficient educational offering into the Hong Kong living room of over-achieving Tiger Moms, you can be sure it will be in for serious scrutiny.

It was not long before parent groups formed at home-gatherings to supplement (/replace) what were proving to be comic-sketch Zoom meetings calling on five-year olds to sit still and pay attention. Some parents would take up the challenge of supplemental schooling themselves, whilst others called upon the wealth of educational talent on the island.

It was (more) fun. And it worked. The engagement was more genuine and interactive. The environment was tautologically more homely.

And it worked out cheaper than the school fees.

What about "socialisation" (cringe).

Well, in Hong Kong, extra-curricular activities were all arranged outside the school and so the kids still played cricket or practised judo with friends in and outside of their learning groups.

The schools struggled to justify themselves. Ours was even introspective enough to try to increase the school fees during this period.

In response to the consequent deluge of lawyerly-bankerish emails that descended upon the admissions coordinator, the school with one hand offered a discount for the next term…and with the other made the passive aggressive point that withdrawing a child for a term would see them at the back of the admissions queue for any subsequent terms.

We were off in any case and for us the question was redundant. But the sentiment was noted.

But the experience added fuel to questions that had already stirred in me about how best to educate the Boys. How to allow them to educate themselves.

I mentioned previously that reading *Free to Learn* by *Peter Gray* had struck a chord. It presented a convincing argument that children are naturally inquisitive and will, given the correct resources and guidance, educate themselves. Allowing them to do this not only allows them to grow into the areas of learning for which they are ready at their own pace but also embeds in them the life-long skills of teaching themselves. Learning to satisfy their own needs rather than being told what to memorise in order to secure an exam grade.

Work Shy

In my mind's eye I would arrive in Montville, get to know people, bounce around and somehow, magically, find a new calling. A lightning bolt striking me with a clarity of purpose for Life – Part II.

All those podcasts, wisely encouraging me (personally!) to take a risk and follow what I believed in, what I enjoy, what I am good at…what makes me unique.

And here I am sitting in a café writing a clumsy memoir. I have peaked into the local jobs market. But there is next to nothing that fits my profile. I am told that in Sydney and Melbourne recruitment agents are now being given female-only mandates – that is they are being told not to include men in their searches.

A light dabble on LinkedIn displays a horrifying stampede of blinkered pen-pushers feverishly desperate to out-virtue each other by barging their destructively myopic, trendy sentiments to the fore. The requirement to fall into line with ESG, Climate, LGBTQIAP+, COVID, Net Zero, D.I.E groupthink is a very real barrier to entry to the 2022 "wokeforce".

Kate is working part time for a company that she was with in Hong Kong. I am struggling with the unique (in my adult life) nagging sensation of spending more than we are earning.

It is a constant trickling of disquiet.

But is it fiat conditioning? What I have been railing against?

In the last 12 months, I have bought myself the most supremely irreplaceable, priceless asset: time. Time with my family. A foundational year in my Boys' childhood. No matter what happens, I am as certain as can be that I won't lie on my deathbed wishing I had stayed in Hong Kong...performing another year's lap of the corporate calendar.

Forthcoming Armageddon and inflation notwithstanding, we will never starve. I have done as much as can be done to shore up our financial future.

I am a fierce, livid sceptic of fiat money and believe in the far greater value of experiences...and living life in, of and for the moment.

Yet I can still feel the incessant Chinese water torture drip-drip of reproach...not matching expenses with income. What is now my routine non-workday used to be a treasured holiday, allocated to condensed enjoyment. An "earned" reward to the self and the family for making the sacrifice of office time away from how we would otherwise have lived.

Kate tells me it's transitional. Writing that makes me hope it is. I hope the transition is to writing. Maybe that's my next story.

With regard to not working in the office, one of the most striking features I have experienced since sliding out of that metronomically familiar elevator for the last time – now over a year ago – is just how little I have missed it.

In the last 12 months, I haven't professionally applied myself in the skills that I had absorbed over the previous 27 years. Not once. And yet I feel no less fulfilled. If anything, I feel more content in my life choices...of having spent so much time with my family.

That is not to say this is a permanent state of peaceful, post-professional piety! There are many occasions, especially when the hungover mind is mendaciously whipping up demons with which to torment the weakened self that my stress levels rise in the realisation that I have amputated a section of my being that was pumping in a generous flow of fiat.

I am still learning to cope with the nagging discomfort of spending money when none is coming in. A sense of depletion in what we have.

It has also made me question how we have found ourselves (it is certainly not just me) in this mindset.

It is hard for us, never mind our children, to conceive of a working life where you shut the door on the third party, career compartment of your life every day of the working week, let alone the weekends.

In my father and mother's era, the 1970s, 80s, 90s, once you had jumped in your death-trap car home, no-one could reach you, even if they wanted to. There was no point thinking about work because you would not be able to communicate that thought to work until 9am the following day.

I know this is oft discussed amongst the office-erati but have we really thought about the pervasiveness, the profound penetration of work in our lives and how this has changed the quality of our existence?

Smart phone emails, first thing in the morning, last thing at night and even over the weekends. A constant nagging tug underlying our daily interactions. A stream of income contingent on sacrificing the foremost, real-time layer of our attention. A numbing of our now-receptor.

A persistent, insistent demand on our thinking time. Time that might be spent thinking about what we want beyond the blizzard we are told we need to yomp through in order to reach the hearth-warmed refuge of retirement.

Maybe if we had time to look – to see - to our left or right we might catch a glimpse of an alternative path off the mountain.

No Pain No Gain

I have always identified in myself the instinct to do something difficult to make sure the reward feels that bit better. A warm shower after playing rugby in the sleet, beers after a painful week at work, a sofa session after a multi-hour hike.

Is that a human condition – innate? Is it genetic or environmental? We all know people who have very little problem rewarding themselves despite not having endured any moments of challenge. Those that are able to enjoy indulgent luxuries despite not having physically earned their worth.

But, for the vast majority of us, being busy is seen to be honourable and virtuous. Is that social conditioning? Or our subconscious reminding us that we are capable of more.

Certainly, when Kate finds me sat quietly on the deck having a think, there is a list of jobs the doing of which raises my virtue as perceived through her eyes!

Being seen to be busy, even to no external benefit, is deemed better than to be doing nothing.

I suppose that's what we are all calling "bullshit jobs". And I can see that. A strikingly common sight in Australia is a set of questionable roadworks manned by a team of workers in "hi viz" day glow vests. A set of temporary traffic lights could perform the work of this football team of (usually bearded) men.

Is this, in reality, Universal Basic Income but in a form that delivers a dopamine reward hit?

Given how much of the Australian economy seems to stem from government, is this roadside scene just a manual worker version of what is more pervasively happening in office blocks across the country?

Of course, arriving and settling into our Hinterland home was never going to be the answer to all our life-living questions. That, inevitably, will be an on-going process. Kate has found her holding position, with a congenial part-time job.

I have deferred the issue by writing this!

Hope and Fears

One of the Daily Stoic podcasts (the narrator is annoying, but I still occasionally make myself listen) talked about the wisdom of writing down our hopes and fears. Of taking stock by crystallising thoughts into the written word. So here goes:

Hopes:

- That the Boys flourish into kind, thoughtful humans with a grounding in nature, thinking for themselves and a clear set of strong principles that will act as guiderails for when times become difficult;
- I would dearly love for my personal combination of skills and passions to click together to open a pathway towards a rewarding use of my time that leaves the World around me at least a little better-off;

Fluffy, as.

- Similarly, for Kate to alight on the people connections that she cherishes between community and our environment.

Fears:

Where to start…FEAR 1)…

1) *Demo-crazy*

I find it interesting how "democracy" is the end point of so many discussions. If we can agree that, "well, that's not democratic" or "hey, that's democracy" then the conversation needs to go no further.

I question that. And, of course, am not the first. Plato believed democracy inevitably led down a path a self-destruction. Questioning democracy was woven into one of Churchill's, a famously broad thinker, most famous quotes. And that was in 1947. 75 years - a lifetime ago. No-one then could have accurately imagined the interconnectedness, speed of communication or technology-driven comfort in which we now live. That was time when the population of the United States was less than 144 million.

In the last few years, our various configurations of democracy across the West have led to:

- UK having three Prime Ministers within two months;
- Germany with Scholtz (who?) leading a three-party coalition;
- France with the choice between Macron or Le Pen;
- Italy having its 66th government since 1945;
- Canada enduring Trudeau based on 33% of a 62% turn-out;
- New Zealand having to listen to Ardern (eek!);
- Australia with the option of Albanese or Scott Morrison; and, of course,
- Our 330 million friends in the USA with option a) Trump or b) Biden.

I will leave Ursula van der Leyen out of the above list because even the most devoted EU technocrat would flunk a polygraph when attempting to describe the process of electing the president of the European Commission as democracy.

The above (other than the polygraph point) are objective facts. My subjective view is that this demonstrates that our democratic structures are failing.

Take the US, ignore the woefully substandard personalities, and simply ask, is it genuinely a realistic proposition to offer 330 million citizens that binary choice – each one of which will drive not only polar opposite but also extremely impactful outcomes on their lives.

When, as the Founding Fathers had envisaged, the president would have a minimal impact on citizens' daily lives…maybe. Even then, no-one was thinking about 330 million people.

But not now. Not when executive orders are flying around like confetti, culture wars are raging and the Fed is printing credit-backed money out of nowhere as if it *wants* to break the system.

May I further subjectively argue that, since our democratic systems have been put in place, our ever more numerous institutions have learned how to game those systems.

Revolving door policies between corporates, governments and regulators, lobbying, political donations, nepotism and indoctrination have all served to contort what were set up as noble structures into a multitude of captive establishments.

In short, our democracies are a sham. But, back to Churchill's "Democracy is the worst form of government, except for all the others". Is that still the case? Winston was talking before we were all so instantly connected. He was also talking from a position of power where he wanted the citizens to OK the democratic structure that had placed him there.

Could new technology be harnessed to make better decisions? The Five Star Movement, which helped form one of Italy's many governments, famously uses online voting amongst its party members to ensure super-democratic decision-making.

But how can the electorate vote on those issues that will inevitably arise that are beyond its competence or ability to analyse? Who decides who is competent for which issues? How does one assess which issues are small enough to avoid a vote? Or too technical to be comprehensible to non-experts?

I am still enamoured with the ancient Greek approach of having minimal government and simply placing capable citizens in positions to supervise the automatic processes of governance for a time-limited periods. Competent individuals were selected by drawing lots. The lack of an election process prevented distraction from the task in hand and the community reward incentive was that of being praised for being as inactive as possible.

Just bloody leave us alone!

However, all that is entertaining speculation. It is impossible to conceive of a process, in today's shockingly divided and entrenched Western societies, whereby a roll-back or new form of government could be devised and to which sufficient consent be provided.

I am sorry to say that I think the rot is so deep that the timbers upon which our current structures stand need to be replaced. Only, as we cannot agree with what to replace them, we are doomed to watch them crumble even as we rely on them to keep us housed.

We will see the demolition of our democracies before we can see new frameworks put in place.

Current policies of governments appear unambiguously designed to expedite that demolition.

And the likes of the WEF are purporting to be the ones to…yes, Build Back Better.

I would rather that the power rested with the people – after all, that's democracy.

2) *Totalitarian Digital Reset*

I refuse to be cowed into meekness on this. Maybe I do have an inclination towards conspiracies. Having lived in Hong Kong where my daily job was to keep up to speed with the plethora of political malfeasance that was deemed standard fare across the Asia Pacific region, I think it's exasperatingly naïve to build a World view on the base assumption that governments are seeking to further human flourishing.

Even if that was how they started out, power corrupts.

So, I fear an authoritarian, digital version of the forthcoming financial reset which itself is inevitable. I have little doubt that we are living during a downward swing in our civilisational cycle. Everybody raves about *The Fourth Turning* by *William Strauss* and *Neill Lowe* but I have to say I found it a stodgy, repetitive read. It was a combination of *The Sovereign Individual* by *James Davidson and William Rees-Mogg* and *The Great Rupture* by *Viktor Shvets* that helped ground my thinking in what I consider to be a foundation of truth.

We have more debt than it is conceivable that we can pay off…as a planet. I recently heard an estimate of US$ 350 trillion. And that was before COVID 19 and the escalation in ESG, renewable mania and the concerted effort to ignore the laws of physics underpinning the necessity of fossil fuels.

At the end of 2019, I was already bleatingly playing Cassandra about how the financial system had never properly taken the required pain to purge the system after the Great Financial Crisis, the GFC. All we had done was to keep the patient alive with the permanent toxic drugs of zero interest rates and "quantitative easing" (read currency debasement / money printing / stealing from the populations).

That was before we locked up the World, printed trillions of USD, the US voted through the Green New Deal, Russia invaded Ukraine, the US defaulted on its fiat reserves with the Russian Central Bank, Sri Lanka decided to ban fertilizers…and then so did The Netherlands and Canada…

Any single one of those developments was enough to tip over the already swaying Jenga tower. And we have experienced them all in 24 months.

It's almost as if those behind these moves want the blocks to fall so that we can all move over to a more modern game…an on-line, virtual game. Political Minecraft rather than Jenga.

No, I am not sure it's the WEF behind it all. Maybe they are a distraction. Maybe there is a clandestine conspiracy behind what everyone has to admit is an open book conspiracy. Klaus Schwab and his sinister Spectre project tells us in no uncertain terms that they view digital IDs, owning nothing, blending the human with the digital as the path they consider to be inevitable for us all.

They don't suggest that we have a transnational debate before we hand over national sovereignty. They openly tell us that they have actively placed their influencers into as many positions of government power as possible. They tell us we will live in city hubs. They say we must eliminate "carbon emissions" by 2050 and stop all reliance on fossil fuels.

None of that is conspiracy. The conspiracy-deniers will say that it is all hot air and that the WEF wields no power.

The same deniers are not aware of striking farmers in the Netherlands and that their prime minister, Mark Rutte, picked up a Global Citizens Award in person from Klaus Schwab. Nor that Trudeau, another WEF darling, is imposing the same restrictions on growing food just as we head into the teeth of a global manmade famine. The worst famine any of us will have seen in our lifetimes.

Famine that will see eye-watering price increases for the majority in the West…but most probably death and starvation for those at the margin in the developing World.

The deniers are good people. They are not denying the truth for personal gain of self-empowerment. They have been socially conditioned to deny "conspiracies".

If it were at all possible…via television, drugs, propaganda…VIA ONLINE SOCIAL MEDIA…would that not be the first agenda item on the list for every wannabe totalitarian power-monger? To deeply ingrain into the population over whom they wish to wield their power that any mere suggestion that they wish to govern over them is a reason for labelling and social ostracization. Othering them as conspiracy theorists.

So, one might say that the WEF is toothless and has no ability to implement the digi-hell that they are imagining. But one cannot say that their vision is a conspiracy. It is there in black and white.

3) *The Spectre of Eugenics*

As a zitty, bum-fluffy teenager I enjoyed crash-testing out loud perilous ideas surrounding genetics with a (mostly outraged) sounding-board chum.

Even then it was a hair-trigger, nuclear bomb minefield.

I am not suggesting that I have any expertise in the matter. But I do have questions.

We have now almost stopped altogether talking openly about genetic matters. So very radioactive is the toxic topic that even the remotest contact could be socially deadly.

As a result, there has been an inverse correlation between i) the knowledge and ever greater god-like capabilities we are gaining and ii) the depth of debate and analysis about how we, as a society, deal with this.

Which is a bit weird. And, just maybe, dangerous?

Or is it not for us to discuss.

Has the topic been deliberately coated in social uranium?

I can quite clearly remember a time, maybe five years or so ago - pre Brexit, Orange Man, COVID, war, etc - when it was pretty much the number one Danger To The World. We had cloned Dolly the sheep. Some Chinese egghead had CRISPRed away HIV in new-borns. Consequently, we had an enormous surge of unsalvable panic over how we could possibly police bucket-brained scientists in North Korea from manipulating genes into birthing an uncontrollable Sinatra-Einstein-Stallone combo. A Frank-Einstein (sorry) super-being.

Would the immensely rich and powerful be able to exclusively commandeer resources in order to genetically sculpt the "perfect" version of themselves? Given that we cannot uninvent the technology and that the World is a multi-governed (currently) patchwork of jurisdictions, how on Earth could we put in place a universally agreed set of guidelines and then enforce them?

The ethical questions take us to the extreme versions of the Trolley Problem. Questions which we, frankly, cannot answer.

Nutty and nasty megalomaniac Genghis Khan famously sired about half of Europe (or something like that). In a global population now 20 times the size, can we really believe there isn't someone sufficiently bananas to seek a similar legacy but without the horizontal huffing and puffing?

But it has all gone incredibly quiet. The CRISPR doc went to jail (he has just been released...at the same time as a new CRISPR technique for HIV has emerged) and the general public has heard next to nothing since. Sinister silence.

Unless, of course, you like conspiracies: it went almost unnoticed that Facebook founder, Dustin Moskovitz ("the face of neoeugenics"), during the COVID event-blizzard managed to obtain an FDA Emergency Use Approval for his Sherlock Biosciences' CRISPR SARS-CoV-2 kit. Creepy!

In my teenage drunken debates, one of the ideas I was kicking around was the forking of humanity. On the whole, is it fair to say the attractive are attracted to the attractive, the intelligent to the more intelligent, sporty to the sporty? Even if it's just a 60:40 bias, over time, might this lead to a polarisation of populations by way genetically-driven characteristics?

"Opposites attracts", I hear you counter. Fair enough. Any maybe that is why we have such a wonderful melting pot World increasingly blending with itself (yes, with a long way to go).

Robert Plomin's *Blueprint* is an eye-opening read of what we know and what we expect to know soon in terms of just how much about each of us is determined by our genetics. He argues that it is scientifically demonstrable that even softer characteristics such as resilience and generosity are largely genetically driven. And that we will increasingly be able to identify those markers on individuals' genes.

But when do soft characteristics become hard?

It is almost standard now for pregnant women in the West to have a screening for Down's Syndrome with a view to potentially aborting the pregnancy if the result is positive.

I don't know. I am genuinely asking the question: is that not an inching down the slope to a form of generic eugenics?

For good or for bad, sure. Some will say we are eliminating Down's Syndrome. Others will say we are eliminating children with Down's Syndrome. We can have that debate.

However, as we continue to develop our expertise in reading the genome, the more genetic tests become available and the more the question will be as to which genetic markers it is acceptable to manage.

If we identify the grumpy, anger, fury, violent, psychopath gene, where is the line going to be drawn on genetic cleansing?

If humans are intrinsically flawed, how can we make flawless judgments over which flaws are, or are not, desirable in our future offspring?

Jamie Metzl framed it somewhat differently in his *Hacking Darwin*. What is to stop the rich elite from IVF-ing 40+ embryos, analysing them for their optimal or favoured genetic profile and selecting that one and discarding the others. Or selecting the best five...or ten...

Could that lead to a bifurcation of humanity - of a super-rich, super-being elite that irredeemably accelerates away from the business-as-usual proletariat? In a generation's time, could we get to the point where you are deemed irresponsible for not having a genetic health check as an integral part of your family planning. Eliminating problematic [define] disorders. Think of the savings for society: less burden on the welfare state, on healthcare...on the legal system, schooling...

But isn't that artificially homogenising the human race? Or at least the portion of the human race with the resources.

I am freaking myself out all over again!

And THAT is the easy stuff.

That's all before you start worrying about the proper sociopaths CRISPR-snipping in a bit of extra resilience here, clipping out a bit of excess empathy there. A little bit taller, a bit cleverer.

A few months ago, scientists finished decoding the entire human genome.

Industry scientists are openly talking about gene-edited babies.

Our recent Western COVID experience suggests that those in government consider themselves empowered and are eager to make fundamental ethical decisions for us without much consultation. And with a fair bit of PR.

It is very noticeable that my hopes are relatively succinct and clear. Whilst my fears are more rambling and open-ended.

CONCLUSION

A trio of quotes from **Pericles***:*

"Just because you do not take an interest in politics doesn't mean politics won't take an interest in you."

"Freedom is the sure possession of those alone who have the courage to defend it."

"What you leave behind is not what is engraved in stone monuments but what is woven into the lives of others."

So – what was all that about?!

The primary purpose of my meandering mitherings is so set out for Rex and Raf my thoughts over the last few years. The scale of change in our World has been beyond comprehension over the course of my lifetime but it is self-evident that developments are accelerating. By the time they read this, the moments in which we made these life-changing decisions will be lost. The context of our thought processes will likely be irretrievably extinguished.

I worry that the retrospective lens through which they read these thoughts will be tinted…tainted - some may say cleansed, so that my views and actions will be condemned.

I hope not.

I hope that Kate and I have lived and brought them up based on a set of principles that will stand that test of time and technology.

I have amateurly peered back into time in an attempt to base those principles on some ancient wisdom. But it strikes me that when Aristotle and the Stoics essentially exhorted that individuals should not concern themselves about problems over which they have no control, they were living in an environment where it was far easier to delineate areas of life where that was obvious.

Nowadays, our interconnectedness has shown that even those from the poorest and most obscure backgrounds are able to have influence on the World around them – sometimes even on a global scale.

Should I give up on trying to change what I see as the abject mismanagement of the World? Does one try to do what one can within the confines of the skewed system in which we live? Is writing an ego-centric memoir of any help whatsoever?

Shouldn't we just focus on the community around us – where we can directly see the impacts (ideally benefits) of the actions we take? Dunbar's number suggests the average's person's cognitive abilities limits them to being able to maintain proper human relationships with only 150 friends and family.

Isn't that essentially how humans are wired to live? Our genetic traits have not had the evolutionary time to catch up with the quantum (literally?) leaps in technology and ability to interact with the planet beyond our village.

To boil it down to the basics, this was what our transition to the rural Sunshine Hinterland was really about.

Living in the Moment

I have not kept track of the multitude of intellectual wisdom bombs purporting to reveal the meaning of life. From "the meaning of life is the search for the meaning of life" (cop out?) to *Viktor Frankl*'s revelation from *Man's Search for Meaning* that it's your reaction to suffering, your connection with your inner "I", that provides ones' purest value.

However, for me what chimes as closest to the truth is that of living in the moment. Appreciating what we are experiencing in the now for its very essence of being.

Sam Harris did a good job of trying to illustrate the idea: he made the point that everything we experience in life can be reframed if we think of it in terms of being the last time we will ever experience it. He drew on the example of your baby crying in the night - how we can transform what is normally a resented, bleary-eyed bumbling in the middle of the night. At some point, there will be a last time that we do that. Our baby will no longer be a baby and no more need soothing at 1.43am. If we think of it as being potentially the last time we ever pick up our offspring, that early-hour chore suddenly reframes itself as being something closer to the essence of life.

Loving the act of loving.

The more we can remind ourselves to look up, take stock and think – think about the indescribable miracle of the experience of living – the more we will find meaning in life being the living of it.

My current thinking aligns with that of Alan Watts; "the meaning of life is just to be alive. It is so plain and so obvious and so simple. And yet, everybody rushes around in a great panic as if it were necessary to achieve something beyond themselves."

This aligns with the decisions we have made as a family.

We stopped rushing around. We moved to an area of profound beauty. Immersed in nature.

I find more time than I can remember in my life, to just sit and enjoy being.

I am insanely privileged to have found the means to get to this point.

Imagine if all those that had the equivalent privilege did the same.

And allowed the capacity for the less privileged to find their meaning also.

If we all thought rather than bought.

Ultimately, that happiness is in your head.

<u>One final quote for Rex and Raf:</u>

"Employ your time in improving yourself by other men's [/ women's] writing so that you shall come easily by what others have laboured hard for."

Socrates

All sides of every argument and think for yourselves, please, Boys!

BIBLIOGRAPHY

Financial System

The Creature from Jekyll Island – G. Edward Griffin

The Bitcoin Standard – Saifedean Ammous

The Fiat Standard - Saifedean Ammous

When Money Dies – Adam Ferguson

Lords of Finance – Liaquat Ahmed

The Price of Time – Edward Chancellor

Principles

The Righteous Mind – Johnathan Haidt

The Rational Optimist – Matt Ridley

How Innovation Works – Matt Ridley

Thinking Fast and Slow – Daniel Kahneman

The Lessons from History – Will and Ariel Durant

Man's Search for Meaning – Viktor Frankl

The Wellspring of Human Progress – Henry Grady Weaver

Aristotle's Way – Edith Hall

Siddhartha – Hermann Hesse

Education

Free to Learn – Peter Grey

The Element – Sir Ken Robinson

Weapons of Mass Instruction – John Taylor Gatto

Thriving at School – Dr John Irvine and John Stewart

Downturn

Disunited Nations - Peter Zeihan

The Fourth Turning - William Strauss and *Neill Lowe*

The Sovereign Individual - James Davidson and William Rees-Mogg

The Great Rupture - Viktor Shvets

Tragedy and Hope 101 – Joseph Plummer

Disorder – Helen Thompson

Genetics

Blueprint - Robert Plomin

Hacking Darwin - Jamie Metzl

Science

The Beginning of Infinity – David Deutsch

The Order of Time – Carlo Rovelli

The Meaning of Human Existence – Edward O. Wilson

Sapiens – Yuval Noah Harari

What is Life – Paul Nurse

Climate

Unsettled – Steve Koonin

Watermelons – James Delingpole

A Requiem for a Species – Clive Hamilton

How to Talk to a Science Denier – Lee McIntyre

The Inconvenient Facts – Gregory Wrightstone

Human Caused Global Warming – Dr Tim Ball

How to Avoid a Climate Disaster – Bill Gates

Fossil Future – Alex Epstein

COVID

The State of Fear – Laura Dodsworth

The Next Great Depression – James Rickards

The Price of Panic – Douglas Axe

The Real Anthony Fauci – Robert F. Kennedy Jr

ABOUT THE AUTHOR

If you made it this far, you know more about me than is comfortable for either of us!

For further rants, please visit (and subscribe?) to my blog on Substack under the pseudonym AngryGnome ["you're right to want the right to be right or wrong so that you can be more right than wrong in the future"]:

https://substack.com/profile/47177471-angry-gnome?utm_source=user-menu

Or visit my website:

www.garethwilliams.com.au

or

www.angrygnome.com.au

CPSIA information can be obtained
at www.ICGtesting.com
Printed in the USA
LVHW041155031222
734485LV00005B/424

9 780228 886150